REAL DADS SAY IT

As a father, it can sometimes be difficult to put into words the most important values and lessons that we want to pass on to our sons as they quickly grow into men. The letters in *I Call Shotgun* are a wonderful tool for any father who is serious about the job of raising men of character. Use these letters as they are written, or use them as a guide to write your own personal letters to your son.

MARK E. CRAWFORD, PHD, LICENSED CLINICAL

PSYCHOLOGIST; FATHER OF 2 SONS; AUTHOR

Actions speak louder than words . . . finding moments to share, to teach, to bond, and to experience life with your children is a critical part of being a father. Curt and Tommy know this fact and their words of wisdom are always laced with great stories that come from the heart and real life. The journey as a father is filled with the unknown. So the principles that guide you are so important. *I Call Shotgun* is a must read for anyone who cares about making the most of his role as a father.

BOB BURDICK, FATHER OF 5 SONS, GRANDFATHER OF 10 GRANDSONS

AND 5 GRANDDAUGHTERS, GREAT GRANDFATHER OF 1

Our society is in desperate need of men of integrity and *I Call Shotgun* is so timely and will equip our next generations of young men with the necessary principles of faith and morals. This is a must read for fathers, mothers, or any-one with a passion to see these next generations of young men grow into their full God-given potential. Curt and Tommy have done an exceptional job of lay-ing out the fundamentals to help these young boys develop into the leaders they were designed to be.

BOB CHRISTOFFERSON, ENTREPRENEUR; FATHER OF 3 YOUNG MEN

As a pediatrician for thirty-eight years I have noticed that fathers are not taking the responsibility of passing wisdom on to their sons . . . this has left a huge void in the quality of character development. *I Call Shotgun* is a sorely needed guide to recapturing true wisdom. I highly recommend it.

J. DAVID WILLIAMS, MD

The wisdom in this book can make a positive impact on anyone. I would recom-mend it to my friends and encourage them to share it with others.

JEFF ROBERTI, #1 WORLDWIDE DISTRIBUTOR, JUICE PLUS+

This is a must read for dads who are raising boys to become men of conviction in a crazy world adrift in confusion about values. I have raised three sons myself, so I always appreciate other men who are as committed to being a great active father figure. Tommy and Curt have provided an amazing and practical handbook for dads raising sons. I love the short chapters and the "street smarts"! In a world trying to drown out the voices of fathers, this is great handbook for fathering.

DR. HANS FINZEL, PRESIDENT OF HDLEADERS; BEST-SELLING
AUTHOR, *THE TOP TEN MISTAKES LEADERS MAKE*

The message that the next generation so desperately needs to hear.

GEORGE PEART, DIRECTOR OF SALES/PARTNER,
GULF STATES ENGINEERING CO., INC.

There are not many subjects more important than fathering. These are not just repeated formulas; they are lessons learned and proven principles. Without hesitation I would advocate this book for anyone who finds himself with a hunger to be better at what really matters, raising up the next generation of fathers.

BUDDY HOFFMAN, PASTOR, GRACE FELLOWSHIP CHURCH

For twenty years I've watched Curt Beavers prove a key biblical principle . . . men can be successful rearing Christ-loving sons. He's earned the right to be heard.

FRED LIVELY, BUSINESSMAN; PROUD FATHER OF
A GODLY UNITED STATES MARINE

I Call Shotgun is a lesson about the truths of caring for, mentoring, and shaping a son . . . life-changing lessons for any father or young man.

KERRY DAIGLE, AUTHOR, *DREAMS, FAIRY TALES, AND MIRACLES*

In this book Curt and Tommy offer valuable wisdom and insights to all fathers on the important role God has bestowed upon us and the valuable lessons we are to share with our sons.

MIKE BREEN, GLOBAL TEAM LEADER, 3DM

I CALL SHOTGUN

I CALL SHOTGUN

LESSONS *from* DAD
FOR NAVIGATING THE ROADS OF LIFE

TOMMY NEWBERRY
and CURT BEAVERS

THOMAS NELSON
Since 1798

NASHVILLE   DALLAS   MEXICO CITY   RIO DE JANEIRO

Published in Nashville, Tennessee, by Thomas Nelson. Thomas Nelson is a registered trademark of Thomas Nelson, Inc.

Thomas Nelson, Inc., titles may be purchased in bulk for educational, business, fund-raising, or sales promotional use. For information, please e-mail SpecialMarkets@ThomasNelson.com.

The Library of Congress Cataloging-in-Publication Data is on file with the Library of Congress

ISBN-13: 978-1-4002-0464-9

Printed in the United States of America

13 14 15 16 17 RRD 6 5 4 3 2

To our boys, Ty, Trey, Mason, Zach, and Brooks; and to all dads committed to raising and influencing high-character young men.

CONTENTS

CONTENTS

INTRODUCTION

Young men hunger to understand, appreciate, and emulate the ideals that reflect who their dads are and what they believe. Teenage boys want to learn and *should* learn the lessons of life from their fathers. But if we neglect this vital responsibility, there are plenty of other counterfeit sources of wisdom that are ready to enthusiastically play the role of surrogate dad for us.

These "alternates" include the mass media, entertainers, and a large chunk of our education system, all of whom are committed, ready, and willing to jump in and fill the void we may leave, and they're ready to teach our boys their version of the lessons we neglected to pass down. This is a real problem, and it is the reason we had to write this book.

Like us, you want your son to become independent, individually responsible, and successful in all areas of life. You want your son to carry forth your values and sustain those ideals into future generations. Unfortunately, there is no playbook for accomplishing this, at least until now.

Since you are reading this book, we assume we have a lot in common. At a minimum, we are confident that you want to equip your son with the understanding and wisdom to succeed in the world today. We wrote this book with you in mind, to help make being an engaged and influential dad a little bit easier. It is our prayer that we will be able to help bridge the gap between intention and reality for you.

I Call Shotgun makes the passing down of traditional values and timeless truths easy and productive. With this book in your hands, you have an organized playbook and clear talking points for systematically communicating the things that matter most to the young men that matter most to you.

These sixty-three hard-hitting and undiluted life lessons present the "street smarts" and practical wisdom every son needs but few receive. You will find this book to be a thought stimulator, checklist, lesson guide, and inspirational handbook all rolled into one.

HOW TO USE THIS BOOK

This book can be read straight through, or you can skip around and read the chapters in any order you desire or choose those that seem most relevant at the moment. We intend for you to take the ideas in this book and make them your own. Using the letters we wrote to our sons as your rough draft, craft your own typed letters and handwritten notes over the coming days and weeks, adding your own perspective and life experience as desired. Mail these letters to your son one at a time or leave them in his room before you head out of town or leave for work so that he'll notice them when he returns home. Start now, today. Do not put this off until tomorrow.

In the back of the book, you will find a special section entitled Conversation Starters. These questions for you and your son are intended to facilitate constructive conversations, inviting each of you to insert your personal experiences into the topics we have covered. We encourage you to write your own questions and make other notes in the margin as you read each letter. To get the most out of it, make *I Call Shotgun* an active read, preferably with a pen or highlighter in your hand. Finally, incorporated throughout the book, you will find text messages designed for you to "borrow" and send to your son periodically. Of course, feel free to make up some of your own as well.

We hope *I Call Shotgun* becomes a legacy resource that empowers you to transfer your real-life values and convictions for the purpose of influencing generations to come.

Our prayer is that these words to our own sons will be an encouragement for you as you strive to raise godly sons, young men who are more inspired and capable of influencing the world around them, rather than being influenced by it.

—Tommy (dad to Ty, Mason, and Brooks)
and Curt (dad to Trey and Zach)

1

DO COURAGEOUS THINGS

Dear Trey,

Throughout your life, you will face times when you are scared. But you will be far from alone. No one is immune to this experience. Both cowards and heroes face fear. Their responses to fear and uncertainty, however, define who they become.

> U are a beautiful, wonderful child of God!

And this will be true for you as well. The really good news, believe it or not, is that you were not born with courage. But neither was anyone else. Why is this *good* news? Because it means that courage, rightly understood, is learnable.

As a man, fear may arise from a physical threat, a strained relationship, or a financial challenge, but it happens to us all. How you choose to face this fear will help define who you become. The more you practice being brave, the braver you will become.

As you develop more courage, more opportunities will come your way. As your courage expands, so too will your depth of character. And this will be apparent to everyone around you.

With courage, you do what's right regardless of what's popular. Sometimes this will mean overtly taking a stand, and other times it will simply mean bypassing the path everyone else is following. You exhibit courage when you stick by a friend after everyone else has abandoned him. Saying no when everyone else says yes shows courage. It also takes courage to stand up for your convictions when everyone else is sitting down.

Son, you must act courageously even when you feel uncourageous. This is a critical point, especially if you aspire to be a leader someday. Those moments when you are faced with the option to either do what's right but difficult or what's wrong but convenient will become the defining moments of your character. I assure you that I regret the times I weakly went along just to get along.

Courage is the opposite of immobilization. It's the guts and grit to do what's right because it's right. Courage is the willingness to launch into a new venture without a guarantee, to risk failure and follow your dream. Every business in America reflects an act of courage. The famed management teacher Peter Drucker once said, "Whenever you see a successful business, someone once made a courageous decision."[1]

Whether you are a student, an athlete, an artist, or an entrepreneur, success requires courage. It takes courage to think independently and rise above the crowd. Acts of courage reveal what you're really made of and set the stage for continuous growth and self-mastery. Living with courage fuels the inclination to get outside your comfort zone and operate in the character zone.

American history is filled with stories of courageous people. It took courage for America's first settlers to get on those ships and sail to the unknown. It took courage for Patrick Henry to declare, "Give me liberty or give me death." It took courage for the Greatest Generation to storm the beaches of Normandy. It took courage for Rosa Parks to quietly refuse to give up her bus seat. It took courage for the first astronauts to launch into unchartered territory. It took courage for firefighters to rush into the World Trade Center when everyone else was running out. It took courage for Captain Sullenberger to safely land his plane in the Hudson River and be the last one to disembark.

Courage is both inspiring and infectious. Become infected with this uncommon quality, son, and as a leader, you will start an epidemic that will rapidly spread and take you to places you never dreamed possible. When others witness your acts of courage, they will be inspired to do likewise. Courage, as the legendary British prime minister Winston Churchill observed, "is rightly considered the foremost of the virtues, for upon it, all others depend."[2]

Build your life upon a foundation of courage, Trey, and be blessed with the strength, character, wisdom, and integrity your courageous choices will bring.

Love,
Dad

2

VALUE YOUR TIME

Ty,

You cannot see it. You cannot alter it. You cannot stop it. But the direction and quality of your life will be heavily shaped by it. I am talking about time—the cumulative moments of your life.

I encourage you to learn to value time early in your life. Many of your friends, acquaintances, and even role models will not understand the value of small moments. They will waste a few minutes here and a couple of hours there, never realizing that lost time accumulates and undermines who they're capable of becoming and the goals they might accomplish.

But as time passes, options diminish. By the time you hit age thirty, you will have observed for yourself many who never appreciated the time they were given and, consequently, squandered opportunities and maybe even years of their lives. As you grow older, you will find that life, with its temptations and distractions, can become noisy and confusing, and you can be easily drawn into wasting your time with lesser things.

How well you manage your life will largely be determined by how well you manage your time. Time management will rarely be easy. You will have to make difficult decisions. You will have to turn down nice people, pass on exciting pursuits, and say no to worthy projects. But the truth is, you simply cannot give your time and attention to every good thing that presents itself to you.

While there will never be enough time to do everything, there will always be the time to do the right things. God hasn't shorted us on time, but he does require that we invest it wisely. Ty, you will find God always provides enough time to accomplish what he wants you to accomplish.

Dad

3

CELEBRATE OTHER PEOPLE'S SUCCESS

Dear Mason,

God created a world where one person's success benefits the people around that person. In fact, our success creates ripples that spread out in circles far beyond us. Like pebbles dropped into a pond, those ripples intersect across communities, cultures, and even generations. God desires that all his children be blessed, and he created an economy based upon our mutual support for one another. By his design, your success blesses others.

But what is success? Many people today define that word by the size of a paycheck, the fanciness of their clothes, the reflections in their mirrors, the size and numbers of their homes, or the measure of their influence. But success is the process of making God's desires our desires and becoming more like he engineered us to be, day after day. Success is God's way of creating abundance in his universe, and he uses our success to help others create success. When we do well, we're able to help others do well. As I've often encouraged you, do well so you can do good!

However, the world today sees success in a different way, as a system of competition built on envy and jealousy. The truth is, Mason, we typically repel what we resent. When you waste your energies on envy, jealousy, and resentment, you block your ability to achieve your own success. God knew that it's not only wrong to break the tenth commandment, "Thou shalt not covet" (Ex. 20:17 KJV), it's counterproductive. He created a world where success is built not at the expense of others but in service to them. In spite of what is fashionably promoted today, success is a multiplier, not a divider.

The flip side of this message is the good news: the fastest way to achieve success is to genuinely admire and applaud the success of others. Our appreciation and gratitude for others' well-being releases a mental switch that draws us toward our own dreams. Only the architect of the universe could author a system where one person's success enables the hopes and dreams of others.

> I love u forever, always, no matter what!

Reinforce this mind-set while you're still young, Mason. Get into the habit of cheering for your friends, classmates, and teammates when they achieve special distinction. This won't always be easy, especially if you were competing with them, but it is a sign of high character and a mental building block to your own future accomplishments.

Imagine that a few years down the road you graduate from college after investing years of hard work. You marry the girl of your dreams and find the job you've always hoped for, and the two of you put a down payment on a house, thanks to having a good income from a business owner who's invested in you to bolster his company's success. Your success blesses him. You bring skills he's been looking for and help him advance his company. And his success blesses you. You're now a homeowner. Based on your contributions to the company, he adds another position.

But the ripples continue. Two real estate agents involved in the sale of your home earn a commission. One pays off his credit card debt. The other agent takes a vacation to San Diego with her husband. The airline generates revenue, along with the San Diego hotels, restaurants, attractions, and the rental car company. Back home, a teenage boy earns some extra money house-sitting while the couple is traveling, so he takes his girlfriend out for dinner and leaves a big tip to impress her. The waitress goes home with a little extra cash that night and sends off some money to her little sister at college who goes out the next day for a long-anticipated manicure. Back home, you're buying rakes, hoses, paint, hammers, and other supplies to fix up your house and giving the neighborhood hardware store a boost.

Long story short: your hard work and success feed the success of others. Businesses profit, families profit, local and state governments profit, and communities thrive. Now multiply this example by 100 or 1,000 or 100,000. Hobby Lobby's founder and CEO, David Green, is responsible for producing 16,000 jobs. Bernie Marcus and Arthur Blank, founders of Home Depot, together have created more than 300,000 jobs. Imagine the exponential influence of their success on millions of lives. These men, and tens of thousands of women and men like them, risk their futures and pour their hearts into serving others through their initiative in a free marketplace. The return on their investment blesses millions by the ripples created through their business success. As a nation and as individuals, we should rejoice in this!

Success creates a cascade not only in the business world but in all walks of life, from school teachers to homemakers to ministers to surgeons to sales people. When we serve others with excellence, ripples of blessing spread far and wide. Never be intimidated or resentful of the success of others in perfecting their crafts or skills, serving others, or creating successful ventures. Cheer them on. Recognize and appreciate people's principled efforts to contribute to the world.

It's never cool to pull people down with criticism or negativity, or to devalue their achievements. Too often people respond to others' success with sour grapes, bitterness, and belittling. But don't fall into this trap, son. This kind of negativity always reflects poorly on the person too emotionally and spiritually shallow to be able to celebrate the success of others. You're bigger than that, Mason. God celebrates the successes of his children, and he calls us to be like him. Celebrate the service, innovation, gifts, leadership, and creativity of others. Applaud the good things they bring to the world. Learn to smile as the cameras flash for other people and to mean it.

Remember, you're secure in God's love. He has a plan for you, and you never have to feel threatened or intimidated by the talents or successes of others. In fact, you should pray for other people to be blessed and succeed. This is what Jesus taught in the golden rule—even as far as loving and praying for the success of our enemies (Matt. 7:12).

If you hope to enjoy greater rewards tomorrow, appreciate those who are experiencing success today. Study their paths to success, and be humble and willing to learn. Ask God to free you from jealousy and envy, and watch your own success grow as you learn to genuinely engage in the success of others.

Celebrating you,

Dad

4

APPRECIATE WHAT YOU HAVE

Dear Brooks,

Never underestimate the power of appreciation for what you've been given. The moment you begin to lose a sense of gratitude, your perspective on life will become distorted and your motives will become entangled in a web of selfishness.

The problem of ingratitude began with our first parents, Adam and Eve. We tend to think Satan tempted them to do something diabolical in the garden of Eden. But when we look at Genesis chapter 3, we see a different scenario. The devil took a subtle approach to introduce sin to the world: he undermined Adam and Eve's confidence in the character of God by tempting them to be ungrateful for all they'd been given, and he planted seeds of doubt about God's goodness.

And it worked.

In one conversation, the fate of the world changed. Adam and Eve forgot what God had given them—life and breath, a world filled with mind-blowing beauty, and most important, free access to him in a loving relationship. Instead, they allowed ingratitude to seep into their hearts. They allowed doubt to fuel fear, and selfish desires to choke out a spirit of worship.

Gratitude is a spiritual measuring stick, son. It's a sign of a man whose heart is tethered to God and whose perspectives are rightly ordered. Gratitude creates a Philippians 4:8 perspective that looks for the true, the noble, the right, the pure, the lovely, the admirable, and the excellent. Gratitude fosters a heart that resonates with the heart of Jesus, who deflected glory from himself and directed it to his Father.

When you experience a sense of gratitude, it means that you have been thinking about the good stuff in your life such as your family, friends, health, and recent accomplishments. When you feel unappreciative, it does not necessarily mean that you are missing something essential. What it does mean is that you recently have been thinking too much about what you don't have and too little about what you do have. You might have been thinking too much about last week's dropped pass in the football game and too little about the A you received on your science exam. You might have been thinking too much about the girl who rejected you and too little about all the other girls.

> God made u 4 something special!

Appreciating our blessings doesn't always come easily. Gratitude is not just an attitude; it is also a skill and discipline to be practiced, especially when we don't feel like it. Gratitude is like a mental gearshift that takes us from discouragement to enthusiasm, from anxiety to inner peace.

The more you appreciate today, the more things you will notice to be grateful for tomorrow. On the flip side, the less appreciative you are today, the fewer blessings you will tend to acknowledge tomorrow. The Greek philosopher Epictetus said, "He is a wise man who does not grieve for the things which he has not but rejoices for those which he has."[1]

The power of gratitude is undeniably immense. As you learn to appreciate what you have, Brooks, praise will become a natural expression of your life. You'll begin to see God's hand everywhere. As your gratitude deepens, you'll find an increasing urge to express that gratitude in praise. In fact, godly, mature men and women understand that life is a continual cycle of gratitude, repentance, and praise.

Godly gratitude will be measured or limited not by what you have, but rather by knowing who you are and who God is. Because this is true, your circumstances can never limit your capacity for gratitude; they can only expand it over the years.

Grow in grace and in the knowledge of your Lord and Savior, Brooks, and unleash the power of gratitude in your life. I have certainly appreciated the privilege of being your father!

Love,

Dad

5

REMEMBER THE WATER SLIDE

Dear Ty,

When you were younger, for six or seven years our family had a tradition of going to Adventure Island water park in Tampa each summer. I know you remember this! You'd climb up the towering stairs, step by step, and until the very last moment, you had the choice to turn back and lose the opportunity to take that exhilarating ride.

Decision making, Ty, is a lot like riding down that waterslide. You have options right up to the point

> Do what's right, no matter the cost!

when you push yourself off of the safety of the platform and launch yourself into the tube. Once you make that decision, the principles of life kick in: cause and effect and automatic consequences. There's no turning back. Or, as your youth pastor put it, "Once you're naked in the backseat, it's too late."

Our lives consist of the totality of our choices that accrue into something special or something ordinary. A successful life is simply the accumulation of thousands of efforts, often unseen by others, that lead to the accomplishment of worthy goals. You and I are where we are today and who we are today largely because of one single factor: the choices we've made up until this moment.

Consider your past decisions. Each one was accompanied by large or small consequences. Each of these consequences then lead to additional choices and subsequent consequences. As your father, I've been confronted by some of the same life decisions as you.

Both you and I have decided to believe some things and to disbelieve other things. We've decided when to study and when to blow off the books. We've chosen what to learn and what not to learn, whom to spend our time with and whom to avoid. We've decided or will continue to make decisions about who we'll date, who we'll marry, whether we'll have children, and what kind of parent we'll become.

We've decided when to accept responsibility and when to blame others. We've decided to persevere and decided to give up. We've decided whether or not we'll drink, smoke, or use drugs. We've decided what to eat or not eat. We've decided to plan exciting goals for our life or just to wing it. We've decided to give in to fear and decided to bravely press on. We've decided to be the best and decided to act like all the rest.

In just the past year, Ty, you made choices every day, every hour, every minute. How might your circumstances be different today if you'd made just a handful of decisions differently ten or eleven months ago? Going forward, how will you ensure your choices move you toward your goals?

Son, most people make decisions by simply reacting to their environments and living in the moment. Here's the result of living without a clear purpose or plan. An estimated 49 percent of marriages now end in divorce.[1] Seventy-one percent of people working today are dissatisfied with their jobs. Two-thirds of Americans are overweight.[2] Four out of ten will get cancer,[3] and every thirty-four seconds, a fellow citizen has a heart attack. Nearly 75 percent of Americans living in the richest, most abundant civilizations in history will retire with insufficient savings, depending upon government entitlement for their survival.[4]

Son, I don't want to you live an ordinary or average life. I want you to be exceptional. I don't want you to expect the least and be satisfied with the mediocre. My hope is that you maximize your full potential and fulfill the divine destiny God envisioned when he formed you and infused life into your very heartbeat.

Sow a thought, reap an action; sow an action, reap a habit; sow a habit, reap a character; sow a character, reap a destiny. I encourage you to meditate on this truth and then leverage the wisdom it contains to create powerful momentum for growth. Down the road one day, you'll look back and be thankful you followed this life-changing advice.

I love you!
Dad

6

SYNC WITH TIMELESS PRINCIPLES

Dear Ty,

One of the reasons I love sports so much is that they're a great platform for teaching life lessons. As you already know, the principles or fundamentals of each sport are called "the basics." In baseball, football, or lacrosse, the team that sticks to the fundamentals most consistently wins the most.

For instance, in baseball, when a team drifts into a slump, sports analysts often describe the poor performance as playing "sloppy ball." This simply means team members have strayed from the fundamentals of winning baseball. Even a talent-packed team of superstars will stop winning consistently when it fails to execute the proper fundamentals. By refocusing on the basics, individuals, teams, and even nations can break out of slumps.

And the simple truth is that this is how life works as well, Ty. When you stop focusing on the basics, you can pretty much expect to fall into a slump. One of my priorities as your dad has been to teach you the fundamental principles of success. I've observed that some kids grow up with book smarts and some with street smarts, and a few with both. However, too many well-educated young men are ignorant about the laws of life and end up suffering the consequences, in spite of their impressive academic credentials.

If we're not aware of consequences, or worse yet, if we choose to ignore them, the principles of life can kick in and become equal-opportunity destroyers. Take gravity, for instance. If no one ever explained to you the nature of gravity and you accidentally stepped off our new two-story deck, you'd fall straight down, never up. It wouldn't make a difference whether you were a really nice person or a really mean person, whether you had straight As or all Cs; you'd still go down. That's how principles work. They're ruthlessly indiscriminate.

> Write it down—make it happen

A principle, though, is much more than a thought or presumption. A principle is an irrefutable truth, rooted in natural law, that has a history of producing predictable results. Today you're bombarded from all directions by bogus principles. If you're not well-grounded and alert, professors and the media can steer you away from authentic principles and toward trendy perspectives on life. Generally speaking, our Sunday school values are being slandered and undermined.

It's my job as your dad to help you establish a foundation built on rock-solid truth, not the shifting sands of an increasingly secular society. When you leave home, I want you to be knowledgeable enough about truth to recognize fiction. Then you'll be equipped to refute confusing theories and preferences with proven principles.

When you align your life with time-tested principles, you experience confidence and optimism for the future. But the responsibility for learning about these principles and living by them is completely yours. I urge you to avoid the popular position of making up your own version or variation of truth and wasting time experimenting with your own invented principles.

Last year, as you were learning to drive, you read a book titled *Ignorance Is No Defense*. That book is a warning to teenage drivers, and the title brilliantly captures an essential truth about life: ignorance of the law is no excuse. We can break man-made laws and frequently escape without penalty. But timeless principles have a way of tracking us down and delivering unpleasant consequences, in spite of our ignorance or best intentions.

As you know, Ty, I've spent my adult life coaching and advising entrepreneurs and their families. Over the years, I've learned far more than I've taught. Most notably, I've observed over and over again that when individuals stray from timeless principles, trouble and adversity soon follow. Unwavering principles preside over every area of your life. Like gravity, these principles are mostly invisible until you violate them. If you attempt to bend, stretch, or otherwise distort these principles, you'll set yourself up for pain and regret.

Be aware of the danger of wandering away from truth, Ty. It's rare for people to abruptly break away from what they believe. They typically drift away slowly, one compromise at a time. The good news is that whenever people align themselves with authentic principles, their businesses and personal lives become more successful, productive, and enjoyable.

God created a world of cause and consequence. He put boundaries in place, and the rules aren't up for grabs. Principles matter most. When you follow basic principles, life is simplified. Follow fads, and life gets complicated. This is true for individuals as well as nations. The quickest way to create a mess is to violate timeless principles. The quickest way out of a mess is to realign yourself with God's principles. No matter how often you abandon them, they remain unchanged and unfailing. Although you may experience the natural penalties of poor choices, the right course is only a decision or two away.

We're all capable of creating messes. No one is perfect. What matters isn't whether we get off track but the steps we take when we realize it. No matter how good your intentions in life, son, at one point or another, in one way or another, you'll find yourself off track. When this happens, always remember, you're just a principle or two away from the right path.

Just look for the point where you turned off in your own direction and you'll know where to place your feet to head back.

Principles matter most!

Love,
Dad

7

WHAT YOU SEE IS
WHAT YOU GET

Dear Zach,

The dominant images in your mind always influence the choices you make and the direction your life takes. When you create positive, healthy images, you steer your life in a positive, healthy direction. When you hold negative, self-defeating pictures in your mind, like when you worry, you steer your life in a negative direction.

Before something is created in the real world, something is first created in the mental world. In other words, before you can hold the tangible result in your hand, you must hold the equivalent image in your mind's eye. For instance, painters must have a vision of what they are painting before their brushes touch the canvas. Architects must create mental images of the homes they design before they develop actual blueprints. A placekicker will first kick a forty-five yard field goal in his mind before he makes it happen on the field. Responsible parents envision their children as successful adults, and this picture guides their decisions along the way.

You too must be able to clearly see what you're striving to create, whether it's a short-term goal or something further down the road in your life. Develop a vivid mental picture of any goal you hope to achieve before you try to accomplish it. Whatever you desire in life, picture it in rich, emotion-provoking detail. Visualize the accomplishment as you drift to sleep at night. Put pictures in your room, in your locker, or on your computer or iPad that trigger your imagination in the same positive direction.

If you intend to move forward as a student, an athlete, or an entrepreneur, first develop a clear, unambiguous picture of what that will look like. Tweak that image. Make it perfect. Hold on to it, and don't let anyone or any circumstance smear that image.

Release the old, outdated pictures that may be swirling in your head, and make room for the new, exciting pictures. Be willing to get rid of old ways of thinking and doing things to make room for your new life. Give up the good to make way for the great.

The words you speak trigger images patterned after them. This insight can save you years of trial and error. Take a look under the hood and listen to your self-talk. What are you saying to yourself? Is your self-talk positive? Does it align with your vision? Does it line up with who God says you are and his goals for you? Positive self-talk is an important step toward creating equivalency between what you envision and how you perform. It can be a powerful force in producing the mental momentum that will draw you toward your goals.

You should be very interested in your future, as you will be spending the rest of your life there. Proverbs 23:7 tells us that "as [a man] thinks within himself, so he is" (NASB). Learn to live with the future in mind, son, and envision your end goal today.

Love,
Dad

8

TREASURE AMERICA'S PERSONALITY

Dear Ty,

Since you were born, I can't remember an Independence Day that wasn't a big deal for our family. Not only are you, Mason, and Brooks out of school for summer vacation, but the Fourth of July is your grandfather's birthday, which makes the celebration even more memorable. Whether we're at the beach or a ball game, you and your brothers have always liked fireworks shows. But the Fourth of July is always special—not just for our family but for all Americans—because it celebrates our freedom and liberty.

Not a day should pass where you don't thank your heavenly Father for the gift of your birth in this great nation. An American heritage means the gift of opportunity, adventure, and blessings for everyone whose eyes are open to opportunity and who are willing to go for it. Unfortunately, many of your fellow citizens don't share a love for our country. Therefore, it's important for me to help you understand what's great and distinct about the United States so you can compare this perspective with the viewpoint of cynics and critics who devalue America.

America's personality is incomparable because its people are unique. As a nation, we are an original masterpiece, a true work of art in progress. We are not a carbon copy of any other country, and we believe this is good. We think independently, and we believe this is good. We express pride in our country because we love what she stands for, and we believe this is good. We have faith in God and high expectations for ourselves, and we believe this is good. We are patriotic, and we believe this is good, because we refuse to forget the enormous sacrifices that were made on our behalf.

As Americans, Ty, we are kindhearted, generous, innovative, driven, fun-loving, forgiving, optimistic, honorable, and determined. As Americans, we believe we are defined by these strengths and not by our weaknesses.

But we also love the unique things that express our American personality, like baseball, hot dogs, and apple pie, of course, but also Miss America and *American Idol*, college football Saturdays and Super Bowl Sundays, backyard barbecues on the Fourth of July and New Year's Eve in Times Square, F-150s and F-18s, Disneyland and Broadway, national parks and Hollywood, rally caps and come-from-behind wins, cowboy boots and country music, Olympic gold and Augusta green, NASCAR and fast cars, self-help and Starbucks, Superman and the "Star Spangled Banner."

And what other country can claim the same quality, quantity, and variety of acclaimed citizens as America? Here are just a few of the eclectic ways our citizens can become household names. You can grow up to become a movie star, musician, professional athlete, astronaut, artist, activist, politician, preacher, military commander, author, radio host, defense attorney, federal prosecutor, corporate leader, entrepreneurial maverick, or even a TV reality star.

> What's Important Now—WIN

And consider a sampling of some of our most notable personalities past and present: George Washington and George Foreman; John Adams and John Travolta; Ronald Reagan and Ronald McDonald; Ben Franklin and Ben Stein; Martin Luther King and Martin Sheen; Marilyn Monroe and Marilyn Manson; Steve Martin and Steve Jobs; Donald Duck and Donald Trump; Larry King and Larry the Cable Guy; Lou Gehrig and Lou Ferrigno. And let's close out the list with Oprah, Madonna, and Diddy. Americans, by and large, reflect intriguing distinctiveness!

But while America undoubtedly has produced more famous people than any other country, from professional athletes to movie stars, our national heroes are also inventors like Thomas Edison and Alexander Graham Bell, explorers like Lewis and Clark, and businessmen like Andrew Carnegie and Michael Dell, as well as everyday people who performed extraordinary deeds, such as Rosa Parks and Todd Beamer. We're proud of our famous sons and daughters, but regular Americans define our unique national persona. Every day millions of citizens from diverse backgrounds chase their own versions of the American dream, and many find it. The lure of the American dream has called out to millions from other nations.

And when America's gates are opened, people flood to our shores to find a home. This, more than anything, tells the world what America is—a place of liberty and justice for all. A land worth fighting for. And a land worth celebrating, not just on the Fourth of July, but all year round.

Love,
Dad

9

WORK HARDER THAN ANYONE ELSE

Dear Trey,

Awhile back, somebody went to a lot of trouble to invent a kind of art called Magic Eye Images. Do you remember the 3-D space shuttle image Nana used to have hanging in her basement? The weird thing about Magic Eye art is that one person can stare at a Magic Eye poster for a few seconds and see a galloping horse or a beautiful sunset, and the person standing next to him can look at the same picture for hours and never find the hidden picture in the tangle of colors and shapes.

Life can be a lot like standing in a Magic Eye art gallery. A lot of people go through life without the vision to see the good things that are right in front of their faces. Those people are the millions in our world who believe work is a curse and something to be tolerated rather than enjoyed.

They're blind to the truth about work. And the simple truth is this: God created his children in his image, and God is a worker. He takes joy in creating. Soon after they were created, God gave Adam and Eve jobs to fulfill in the garden of Eden. Work was part of his design to bring joy and fulfillment. God never intended for us to be bored and miserable from nine to five. He wants us to take pleasure in work. In fact, we should be ready and willing to work harder and better than the person next to us. And why? For the sake of excellence—because excellence both mimics and glorifies God.

Just observe his creation and you'll see that God loves excellence. The human heart beats about forty million times a year with no days off; and although the human brain weighs only three or four pounds, it contains about one hundred billion neurons,[1] which happens to be about the same number of stars as inhabit our galaxy. God made each individual person with the utmost precision. Just look at our DNA. If transcribed into English, the DNA in a single human cell would fill a thousand-volume set of encyclopedias of approximately six hundred pages each.[2] The average adult carries with him about one hundred trillion cells in various sizes and shapes,[3] and with different functions and life expectancies. And consider that the moon is positioned just the right distance from earth to control the tides and prevent us from needing a really big boat!

God made the world excellent, and he intended us for excellence as well. From Proverbs through the parables, God loves excellence, prudence, and productivity. God invented work because it's good for our souls. And because God gave us responsibilities before man messed things up in the garden, we can expect to continue this stewardship in heaven. We will not be passive. Give this some thought. Work is part of what we do to worship him, to extend his creation, and to mirror his image.

You were also created to serve other people. Trey, the greatest joy you'll ever know will be linked to your influence in people's lives. If you listen to God's whisper, you'll realize he created us with a desire to mend the broken and make the world a better place. I want you to feed your motivation to better the world, and push yourself to work harder, love better, and give more. I assure you, if you focus on the giving, the getting will take care of itself. Remember, work is your ministry. And work is anything that you are called to do at the moment. This could involve helping your mom and me, schoolwork, football practice, or a summer job.

No matter what that work may be, do it with a passion for all the world to see. What you do today matters in eternity. When you're on the lacrosse field, work as though God is your coach. When you're studying, work as though you'll be turning your assignment into God, not your teacher. When you're lifeguarding in the summer, know that God is your real boss, no matter who signs your paycheck.

One look at creation shows God's love for excellence. He calls us to reflect that excellence in *everything* we do. The Bible is quite blunt about this: "Whatever your hand finds to do, do it with all your might" (Eccl. 9:10 NIV). I know you recognize those words as that particular verse has been recited often in our home since you were very young. "When you eat or drink or do anything else, always do it to honor God" (1 Cor. 10:31 CEV). Working with all your might means pouring everything you have into everything you do—whether that's your schoolwork, your job, household chores, athletics, or anything else. With all your might means with all your forethought, with all your effort, and with all your conscientiousness.

"With all your might" also means working smart or making sure that you have selected the right work in the first place and are completing it in the right way at the right time. Make the distinction between activity and effectiveness. It is possible to wear yourself out with busywork without being effective. When you are effective, you are making progress toward a specific goal. Working hard is more about doing whatever it takes to produce an excellent result. While this is virtuous, I'll warn you that one of the biggest wastes of time is doing something well that need not be done at all.

The word *always* in the scripture above is clear. Let excellence drive you in everything. Work harder than everyone you know—not to defeat others, but to better yourself and bring honor to God. Compete against yourself to see how much more value you can bring to your team, to your school, to your church, to your friends, to your future marriage, to your community, and to the world.

Hard, smart work and undiluted commitment to excellence are the main ingredients for achievement. Most essential, though, is your motive to do all to the glory of God. You have what it takes!

> Love you,
> Dad

10

SEEK GOD FIRST . . . EVERY DAY

Zach,

Some dads say that their families are important, but then spend very little time with them. Some wives say their husbands are really important, but then spend very little time taking care of their marriages. Many teenagers say college opportunities are critical, but then spend very little time studying. Some people say that their health is a big priority, but then spend very little time exercising their bodies. Many people also say their relationship with God is the most important thing in their lives, but then spend very little time growing that relationship.

Talk is cheap, Zach.

Life is a battle of priorities. We can figure out what is truly important to people by observing how they use their time. It is not what people say or intend to do that reveals their priorities; it is only what they actually do that demonstrates where their hearts are. When it comes to priorities, it is hard to argue that anything else is more important than your faith, right?

But it is not enough to merely have good intentions. If you're going to "seek first the kingdom of God," as we're taught in Matthew 6:33 (NKJV), then doesn't it makes good sense to schedule at least a little time with your Creator first thing in the morning? When your first interaction of the day is with your heavenly Father, your day is established upon the rock of his truth. If there is a more compelling reason to wake up a little early, I don't know what it is.

One of the most life-shaping habits you can develop is waking up early enough to invest time with your Creator before you get fully engaged in your day. This seems like a pretty easy thing to do, but it is actually rather rare. I know the idea of getting up even earlier than you already do is not all that appealing right now, but it really doesn't get any easier as you get older; now is the time to establish the habit. It might be as little as ten or fifteen minutes, but it makes a huge difference. Connect with the Lord before you get busy with the school stuff and before you have tossed your attention to the various other activities and obligations of the day.

The early-morning hours are ideally suited for prayer, Bible study, and personal thinking time. Even though you may be a bit groggy, your mind is clear, relaxed, and receptive to insight and inspiration. In just a few minutes, maybe right before or after you take your shower, be still and remind yourself that God is in control. Read the Bible for a few minutes. Complete a devotional passage. Pray for the day and for your life and for all those you love and also those difficult people in your life. Contemplate the size and scope of God. Remind yourself that any problem is small when compared to your heavenly Father. Thank God for what he is doing in your life and thank him for being with you everywhere you go, from classes to practices to parties and everywhere in between.

Take time every single day to resurrender and open every corner of your life to him. There is no better example of living on purpose and putting first things first than making this morning time with God a nonnegotiable daily priority. You'll often be tempted to skip this time, but discipline yourself to put first things first. After all, what other activity could you claim to be more important?

You will never know how different your day might have been had you skipped this most valuable time together. Since he created you and the universe, why not let him help you create your day? Investing this time first thing in the morning is a single discipline, but it carries with it multiple rewards including insight, strength, wisdom, and peace of mind.

Additionally, you'll move on with the rest of your day with the confident assurance that you have, for today, sought first the kingdom of God. Think about it.

Love,
Dad

11

FOLLOW TRUE NORTH

Brooks,

You have heard me say this over and over again: just because everyone is doing it, doesn't make it right; and just because no one is doing it, doesn't make it wrong. Night after night during your childhood, we have thanked

> Make 2day exceptional!

God that you know what's biblically right from what's biblically wrong. In other words, we gave thanks that you understood "True North," the reference point from which you can navigate your life. We also prayed that God would supply you with the courage to do what's biblically right, especially at those crucial moments when you are the only one choosing to do so.

The world I am trying to prepare you for tends to view truth like a bungee cord, as something that can be stretched in all directions to fit the current moment. Right and wrong are defined more often in terms of what feels good or what feels right to the individual, or, in many cases, what doesn't offend someone else. More precisely, universal truth designed by our Creator has been replaced with personal truth, something people invent for themselves and later edit to fit changing circumstances.

Christian philosopher Ravi Zacharias wrote, "The hollow

lives that fill countless news stories or live in anguished silence reveal the price paid for the belief that truth as a category does not exist."[1]

The True North principle, however, insists there are still fixed truths of right and wrong, despite the sea of moral relativity that now surrounds us. Some of these obvious truths include the Ten Commandments and the golden rule. These traditional markers of True North represent just a fraction of the boundless wisdom contained within the Scriptures. Please remember that rejecting these truths will not block their impact on your life.

These absolute truths, rooted in the Bible, also make up natural or God's law from which the framers of the Constitution established our republic more than two hundred years ago and from which godly lives continue to be built today. For example, the natural law "Thou shalt not steal" (Ex. 20:15 KJV) translates into the natural right of private property and ownership. The natural law of free will translates into the natural right of individual liberty. The natural law of sowing and reaping translates into the natural right of freedom to earn and acquire through personal initiative. These principles are as valid today as ever. How we apply them must surely change, but principles don't have expiration dates.

The fact that many with celebrity status or political influence deny these roots doesn't change the fact that they are the very foundation of our freedom as a people, as well as the foundation of our character as individuals.

Clearly, the further we have distanced ourselves from these fixed truths, the more morally lost we have become as a nation, while our societal, cultural, and political problems have multiplied. To the degree that we line up our choices to be in harmony with biblical truth, we experience predictable success and satisfaction. To the degree that we ignore or compromise on True North, we experience frustration, underachievement, and inevitable regret in the long run.

I want you to be successful. Your heavenly Father does as well. Know what you stand for, and even more important, what you won't fall for; then defend your convictions. It is not enough to know True North; make a commitment to follow it!

Dad

12

ASSUME A GIFT IS HIDDEN

Dear Mason,

British psychologist Richard Wiseman has studied "lucky" people and made some interesting findings. What we often see as a roll of the dice in life is often far more than luck. We actually have the capability to develop power-producing attitudes that can influence the direction of our lives.

One of these attitudes is the expectation that good things are hidden in challenging and difficult circumstances. People with "lucky attitudes" assume that gifts can be found everywhere. If they don't immediately see the new opportunity or advantage, they keep looking. They persist in the face of failure and transform negative experiences into positive ones. Where other people see closed doors, they see possibilities.

The apostle Paul gives us an example of this when he wrote from the Mamertine Prison in Rome. He was chained to a stone floor in a cold, dark, underground cell that was so damp he could never dry out. Prisoners were regularly tortured and executed in the lower cell. But what did Paul do as he waited for his execution? He wrote letters to encourage other Christians. Instead of focusing on his horrible circumstances, he invested his time in serving others.

You can always find gifts in hard circumstances if you're willing to look for them or create them, Mason. Disappointing circumstances often open doors to new opportunities. They force you to think in new ways and to collaborate. Your disappointments also provide coachable moments and give you insight into yourself that wouldn't come if everything were going smoothly. James 1:2–3 says you're to consider it joy when you face hard times because trials develop perseverance, and perseverance produces character.

The great success writer Napoleon Hill wrote, "Every adversity, every failure, every heartache carries with it the seed of an equal or greater benefit."[1] And Alexander Graham Bell said, "When one door closes, another door opens; but we so often look so long and regretfully upon the closed door, that we do not see the ones which open for us."[2]

So as you go through life and doors close ahead of you, and you face setbacks and disappointments, look around you for the hidden gifts. They're waiting for you, if only you have the vision to see them.

Love,
Dad

13

WHATEVER YOU WANT, MAKE A PLAN

Dear Mason,

You and I can learn from the past, but we can't improve it. We can no more change what happened this morning than we can change what happened to you or me in the second grade or to the world on September 11, 2001. But the influence we can have on our future is almost unlimited.

As I've taught you for years, Mason, having a plan for your future distinguishes you from people who say they want great results but have no clear path to reaching their goals. Making a thoughtful, tangible plan for your future shouts to the world that you're a serious participant in your own life. It shows you're a player on the field, not a spectator in the grandstand of life. Planning encourages self-reliance, sharpens critical thinking, diminishes risk, and encourages excellence. It requires you to apply self-discipline and at the same time hones your self-discipline skills for the future. Your first step in planning for your future is always clarifying your destination.

> With God's help, u r unstoppable

Planning is a mark of leadership. Football coaches prepare and guard their plans for every game of every season. Military leaders develop battle plans before executing their assigned missions. CEOs craft plans to grow their businesses in order to outsmart their competition. In fact, most business owners are not allowed to borrow large sums of money from the bank without first filing a business plan.

A plan is a list of action steps or directions for getting from your current location to your desired location. And no matter how logical it may seem to plan before you begin something important, it's easy to be overconfident and rush ahead. But planning will help you get to your goal more efficiently for several reasons. It will help you preview the future and figure out how to bridge the gap between where you are and where you'd rather be. Elaborate, highly detailed plans can be valuable for certain goals; but a short, simple plan is always better than no plan at all.

Things rarely improve by themselves, Mason. If you want next year or your next exam or your next season to be better, you must make changes today. First, make a better plan, and then watch a better life unfold. Hope is not the same thing as a plan, and action without sufficient planning causes frustration and failure.

You and I have often plotted our course using Google Maps or the MotionX–GPS on my iPhone. Once we plug in the end destination, the computer shows us the best route, the street names, distances, locations, and turns. It's pretty simple. Planning is like developing turn-by-turn directions for your life, except that we can't always see a route to our goals. This is why we need to exert the extra time and effort to think ahead.

Planning epitomizes individual responsibility. Why invest the time and effort to plan if someone else is in charge of your life? Planning says you know where you're headed and you're committed to your goal. It says you're proactive and not reactive. It says you're willing to sacrifice because you see the bigger picture. As a planner, you will be in the minority, but don't let this deter you. Most people aren't willing to sacrifice the time or energy necessary to plan how they can most effectively get from where they are to where they'd rather be.

I've observed thousands of people over the years, and I've concluded that irresponsible individuals "wing it" through life. Give this some thought. Most adults want to earn more money, but they have no plan to accomplish that goal. Others want a better job, but they have no plan either. Many single people want to be married to the person of their dreams, but they have no plan. Most married couples want to improve their marriages, but they have no plan. Get it?

Most miserable people want to some kind of significant improvement in their lives, but they have no plan to bring about that change. Sure, they have good intentions, and maybe even a few solid ideas bouncing around in their heads; but in the absence of a well-developed, written, concrete plan, most people continue to do the same things indefinitely and, consequently, create the same outcomes over and over again.

Eventually, they either settle for what they have or become bitter, or quite possibly both. You see, planning takes time, initiative, hard work, and concentration, and it can be emotionally draining. Most people are simply too spent in the distractions of the moment to invest in their futures.

More than anything else, Mason, planning sharpens your thinking. Planning raises tough but necessary questions, but don't let this discourage you. The process of planning triggers ideas and prepares you to respond more constructively to whatever comes your way. Planning prepares you to handle life's eventualities better than you would without planning. Planning allows you think ahead and create strategies. It harnesses your mind power in a singular direction. And don't be surprised when your planning rarely unfolds as you envision it. Planning never means you'll see perfection. But perfection isn't the goal. So remember to begin.

Day after day, year after year, individuals wake up and launch into frenetic activity with little or no vision of how their to-do lists fit in with the rest of their lives. As a coach, if someone tells me they're dissatisfied with some aspect of his life, I ask him bluntly, "What's your plan?" Whether he wants to get into better shape or land his dream job, I ask the same question.

- Do you want to get lean? What's your plan?
- Do you want to earn more money? What's your plan?
- Do you want to raise kids with high character? What's your plan?
- Do you want to have a stronger marriage? What's your plan?
- Do you want to leave a positive legacy? What's your plan?

How about you, Mason? Do you want to make better grades? What's your plan? Do you want to earn more playing time on the lacrosse team next year? What's your plan? Do you want to develop new friendships? What's your plan? Do you want to grow your faith in Christ? What's your plan?

Your plans should begin with the future and track backward. Where do you want to be at the end of your life? Where do you want to be at the end of next year? Where do you want to be at the end of next semester? Where do you want to be at the end of next week? What do you want to accomplish by end of the day tomorrow?

Remember when you were younger and wanted to earn a starting position on the football team? First, I asked you to find a football picture that symbolized your goal. Then you wrote down your goal and attached a deadline. Then you made a list of all the reasons that particular goal was important to you. Next you wrote down everything you could do over the next eight months to be at your best when football camp rolled around. In a few easy steps, you created a simple plan.

Planning is the deliberate act of pulling the future into the present so we can do something about the future before it happens to us. Planning means evaluating your life in light of where you've been, where you are now, and where you intend to go. This is true for an individual, a team, a marriage, or an organization.

A few years ago I was a guest on a radio program where the topic was success and the Bible. Another guest remarked that if we want to make God laugh, we should show him our five-year plan. I quickly added a counterthought: if you want to make God cry, tell him you have no plan at all.

Planning creates opportunity and opens the door for spontaneity. Failure is what happens when we fail to plan. Choose to plan, son. Pull the future into the present and watch the doors of opportunity open.

Love,
Dad

14

LEARN HOW TO READ THE BIBLE

Dear Trey,

As far back as you can remember, the Bible has been part of your life. When you were just a tiny baby, your mom and I read Bible stories to you. You learned the story of creation and Adam and Eve, of Noah and the great Flood, Abraham, Moses, King David, and Job, Solomon and baby Jesus, Jesus' life as a carpenter, his death on the cross, and his resurrection.

We took you to church and taught you the principles of the Bible and tried our best to reflect those principles with our words and actions. When you got a little older, we had quick morning devotions together each day before school, and soon you started memorizing Bible verses. Everything your mom and I have devoted our lives to—our faith and purpose—is anchored in the unchanging truth of the Bible.

The Bible is not just an important book that gives us the principles for our faith. It's God's Word, unlike any other book ever written. It holds the truth for every deception, hope for every problem, perspective for every culture, comfort for every hurt, and a Savior for every sinner.

Some people today read the Bible looking for answers that suit their circumstances instead of looking for what God really has to say. They can take passages out of context, ignore the culture in which the Bible was written, and disregard the big picture of Scripture. We must be willing to be students when we read the Bible and study, not just skim the surface to look for what we want to see and hear. When you were younger, I could read the Bible for you. Now that you are becoming a man, this privilege and responsibility is yours. It will be up to you to read and study the Word of God and incorporate what you learn into the way you live your life.

So how should you read the Bible, son? It's exciting for me to tell you about this, because I believe that the Bible holds the key to successful living for everyone in every generation. The apostle Paul wrote to Timothy and told him that all Scripture was important for

> Actions have consequences!

spiritual growth—that it was inspired by God and profitable for doctrine, for reproof or discipline, for correction, and for instruction in righteousness, so that we might become mature men and women of God (2 Tim. 3:16).

So one of the most exciting ways to read the Bible is to look at the stories of men and women from all circumstances and walks of life to find timeless life principles that show how they responded on their journeys of faith. These principles apply to life today, to every culture and stage of life. The Bible is relevant and timeless.

It's also helpful to see the Bible as God's love letter to us. From the beginning of time, he's been mapping out a plan to save his children. The Bible is his unfolding story of a Father coming after his children who are lost. Although the stories can be challenging, we can better understand the heart of God for us when we see Scripture as God's love letter to us, in chapters that reveal his enduring love.

There are many helpful Bible-reading guides available, and you should experiment with different approaches and study the Word of God from different perspectives throughout the course of your life. Any time you read the Bible, you should first prepare yourself with prayer. Ask God to open your heart and mind to what he wants to say to you through Scripture. Ask him to inspire you and speak clearly to you. As you read, pay close attention to the words, going as slow as necessary to make sure you are truly reading and not just seeing words on a page. I've found it helpful to ask these three questions:

1. What does this mean?
2. What does this mean to me?
3. What am I going to do about it?

I pray that you come to treasure God's Word, son. My deepest hope is that you not just read it but that you love it, obey it, and value it as your most cherished gift from your loving heavenly Father.

Dad

15

ASK FOR WHAT YOU WANT

Brooks,

One of my mentors provided me with a simple way to reinforce this vital point. He said, "If you don't A-S-K, you won't G-E-T." Some call this the asking principle. While a few good things just flow our way in life, we generally have to ask for most of what we want or get used to living without it.

Great coaches ask their players to give it their best. Great CEOs ask for peak performance from their employees. Great salespeople ask the prospect for the sale. Great politicians ask for our votes. Wise young men ask older people lots of questions.

Winners ask for advice. Winners ask for proven methods. Winners ask for the best price. Winners ask for a shot at the starting spot. Winners ask for opportunity. What have you asked for recently?

What we ask for can reveal a lot about us. Asking for help can demonstrate both wisdom and courage. Most really successful people asked for help along the way. Asking doesn't mean you are weak; rather, it means you are smart enough to know that you can't do it all on your own.

For example, there is not even one person walking the planet who knows everything about anything. We are all ignorant in one way or another. When you think about this, it makes you realize that we all are going to need help, information, or insight from someone else sooner or later. The people you may need to help you may spontaneously offer up their support or ideas, but it is far more likely that you will have to ask or go without.

Avoiding asking for what you want can signal fear of some kind. Usually, it is the fear of rejection, or fear of hearing the word *no*. But if you don't ask, you are guaranteeing rejection. Why would you ever do that? Why assume your request for ideas, money, counsel, or collaboration will automatically be turned down? Why assume she won't want to go to the dance with you? Why assume the coach won't give you a second chance? Why not assume the opposite?

U have loads of potential!

The mind-set you have prior to asking often determines whether or not you succeed with the "ask." If your self-talk is pessimistic and self-defeating, you are likely to balk and not even ask. But if you do ask, the person you are asking will detect the insecurity in your tone, facial expressions, or overall demeanor, and the result of your asking will mirror your feeble attitude.

Don't fill your mind with rotten questions like, *What if she says no?* or *What if they reject me?* or *What if I am turned down?* or *What if I don't get the answer I want?* Refuse to take rejection personally. Sometimes it will be personal, but refuse to take it that way!

There are all sorts of reasons people either can't or won't help when you assumed they could and would. It might be timing, competing priorities, or a mysterious circumstance that you will never figure out.

Don't just sit around waiting for what you want; ask for it. Ask her out. Ask for the business. Ask for the raise. Ask for help. Ask for counsel. Have the guts and self-confidence to ask for what you are worthy of receiving. And when you ask, ask with the confident assurance that you will receive. Confidence, not insecurity, nudges the giver toward giving.

Don't beat around the bush either. Those who are in a position to help you will almost always appreciate a precise request over a vague request. Finally, ask early and ask often. Become a serial asker. Ask respectfully, confidently, and repeatedly. Sometimes the "yes" will come after the first attempt, but it is more likely to take multiple tries. Obviously, the more important the ask, the longer you should persevere.

Finding the love of your life, landing that dream job, launching into your own business, and buying your first home will all likely require a great deal of asking. If you are bashful in your asking, you may end up settling for far less than you hoped. If you are bold in your asking, you may end up enjoying far more than you ever dreamed.

Will you give this some serious thought?

Dad

16

REVERE OUR FOUNDING PRINCIPLES

Dear Ty,

We have talked about the special responsibility of honoring the founding principles of our nation since you were very young. When you came into this world, you were immediately the beneficiary of many blessings, foremost among them the privilege of being born on American soil. Many people downplay the significance of this privilege and take it for granted, much as a spoiled child never appreciates the gifts he already possesses.

As a young American who enjoys the privileges this nation has given you, you have a duty to learn about and advocate for the principles upon which this country was founded. After all, if you and your generation can't or won't defend our founding virtues and principles, the America you and your children and grandchildren experience will, by default, deteriorate into something far inferior to the gold standard our Founding Fathers established for us.

If you as a young leader don't know what America stands for, you're likely to sway in the winds of popular political trends. I have tried to keep you informed and talk with you about the issues grown-ups are discussing and debating. I have wanted you to be well informed about the hot issues of the day—from religion to politics and everything in between.

But I also need to know I've given you a solid understanding of the principles that make our nation unique. If you and your generation understand these truths, you will be better equipped to counterbalance the distorted versions of history presented in many schools and on most college campuses. To defend your convictions, you need to know why you believe what you believe and why it matters, especially to your future. So hang with me here for an overview of what we've talked about so many times.

What are u most grateful 4?

The starting point is for you to understand that the Founders of our nation were highly educated students of history, philosophy, and the Bible. They distilled their knowledge into a brilliant Constitution that codified the workings of the entire American government in a document of only ten pages, including the first ten amendments that form the Bill of Rights. They designed our constitutional system to severely limit the government's power to meddle in the affairs of individuals.

These visionary men wrote the Constitution to restrain the nature of man, namely, future government leaders. George Washington painted a clear picture of the dangers of political excess when he said, "Government is not reason, it is not eloquence—it is force. Like fire, it is a dangerous servant and a fearful master." The Founders knew from the Bible that human nature cannot be changed, and they knew from history the disastrous results of believing otherwise. Therefore, they exercised great caution when they allocated man's authority over his fellow man. Because they recognized the failings of human nature, they formulated a system of principles in which both the government and citizens would be accountable to law. As Thomas Jefferson wrote, "Let no more be heard of confidence in man, but bind him down from mischief by the chains of the Constitution."[1]

The Founders were also wise enough to create a constitutional republic, not a democracy. This means the president and lawmakers must govern within the limits and laws of the Constitution to ensure personal liberties are preserved. This representative government avoids the opposing extremes of either mob rule or authoritarianism. Remember, you pledge allegiance to the flag, "and to the republic for which it stands."

Even more important, our Founders knew human rights are God-given and therefore "inalienable." Our individual rights such as life, our pursuit of happiness, our religious convictions, our property rights, and our right to govern ourselves are not granted by man but by "nature's God," according to the Constitution, and cannot be taken away by the government.

The Founders also established self-government. Well aware of the dangers of a cumbersome, oppressive, and centralized government, they wanted power kept as close to the people as possible. In order to self-govern, the Founders envisioned a virtuous and self-reliant citizenry. They considered this to be a prerequisite for successful and lasting self-government. They upheld Judeo-Christian virtues that included honesty, prudence, courage, personal responsibility, private charity, service, hard work, and thrift.

The Founders created a limited government in order to minimize the reach and meddling of the federal government into the business of the states and matters of individual citizens. This choice now stands in stark contrast to our currently bloated and massively inefficient government that continues to grow day by day.

To safeguard us against tyranny, the Founders orchestrated the separation of powers. This disperses and balances government authority between the legislative, executive, and judicial branches.

The Founders also promoted free enterprise, which means individual citizens voluntarily exchange goods and services without governmental interference. The prospect of profit drives innovation, supply, and quality. Prices are determined by competition, not by centralized government planners and regulators.

Because it was essential to free enterprise, the Founders insisted on the sanctity of private property and gave government the task of protecting individual property rights and enforcing contracts. Private property, of course, refers to your land, your home, your car, your money, and any other possessions.

The Founders wanted equal opportunity for Americans, not equal outcomes. It is important to note that equal opportunity does not mean perfect opportunity. Every virtuous citizen was meant to have a shot at creating and experiencing their own version of the American dream. Liberty, the Founders knew, breeds inequality of results. Just because everyone had a shot at the American dream didn't mean everyone would end up with the reality.

Understand that our nation was founded upon a set of ideals, an unprecedented vision that was not instantly fulfilled at its start. The blatant contradiction to these ideals was the existence of slavery in America. You are likely to meet or be taught by those who believe that this inconsistency wipes out all virtue regarding the launch of this country. However, this great flaw does not erase the wisdom inherent in the principles upon which this America was founded. Many of our founding fathers, most namely, Thomas Jefferson, George Washington, and James Madison, owned slaves. Many others such as Benjamin Franklin, John Jay, Benjamin Rush, and

John Adams did not. Even in their hypocrisy, the founders knew that human slavery violated the self-evident truths of individual liberty. Despite inheriting the institution of slavery, our founders established and promoted a central principle—that all men are created equal and endowed with unalienable rights—and this understanding served as the central ideal that would guide and eventually abolish slavery and other violations of natural rights.

Dig deeper, Ty, and do your own research. Become an expert in the history of your country and the divinely inspired principles that make it unique. You and your generation have been burdened with massive debt and threatened by an eroding moral foundation.

But all is not lost. The game is not over. By mastering and becoming a passionate advocate for these critical principles, you will help bring about a Constitutional comeback for the nation. You can make a difference. Be part of the solution, and recruit your generation to join you!

Love,

Dad

17

THINK BEFORE YOU SPEAK

Zach,

If you want to see the character of a man, watch how he speaks at an athletic event—especially if his son is on the court or field. Often we let our emotions control what comes out of our mouths and don't take the time to think about the implications of what we're saying.

We all can look back on life and regret things we've done. But I can promise you that you'll never regret taking the time to think before you speak. The reality is that we often create more problems with our tongues than we do with our actions. Proverbs 13:3 tells us that if we can control our tongues, we'll improve the quality of our lives. This is because what we say has the power to tear people down, ruin their reputations, scar their self-esteem, and wreck relationships.

In Proverbs 18:21, we are advised that both life and death are in the power of the tongue. The words we say to others carry the power to encourage or discourage, to motivate or deflate, to build up or tear down. It's easy to say things in anger and later wish you could take them back. But, once spoken, words cannot be deleted from memory. Get into the habit of watching your words now, when you're young.

Down the road a few years, when you are married and become a father, this will become an even more important practice. Proverbs 15:23 reinforces this truth, "A man finds joy in giving an apt reply—and how good is a timely word!" (NIV). Your words are incredibly powerful, and like seeds, once spoken, they begin to take root and grow wherever they were planted. Positive words bless others. Negative words curse others. It is as simple as that.

In Philippians 4:8, we're advised to keep our minds fixed on things noble, excellent, lovely, and praiseworthy. This applies equally to our mouths as well. Speak with love. Speak with wisdom. Speak as though God is in the room. Use your words to build people up, not tear them down. A man of integrity takes the time to be sure his tongue, his heart, and his mind are all in agreement. Remember this!

Love,

Dad

18

MEMORIZE BIBLE VERSES

Dear Mason,

Every day the world bombards you with messages. You're told how to dress, what to buy, whom to vote for, what to believe. Everyone seems to have something to say about what you're supposed to think.

But amazingly, most people don't filter the hundreds of messages that pour into their minds every day. They seldom apply a grid of discernment to determine what's valuable, what's harmful, what's worth keeping, and what needs to be tossed.

One of your most important jobs in life is controlling your thought life. But how do you do that when the world around you pours in an endless stream of mixed messages? The answer is simpler than you might think. Your most powerful tool in gaining discernment will always be to memorize Scripture. Your greatest asset is God working in you and through you, and this is best accomplished by allowing God's Word to abide in you and shape your attitude and worldview.

Why? Because your mind can only hold one thought at a time, either positive or negative. You can eliminate negative thoughts and lies by substituting positive thoughts and truth. Consequently, memorizing Bible verses is the simplest and surest method for cleansing, renewing, and strengthening your mind.

As you memorize the Bible, you etch Scripture permanently in your mind, where it abides in you and unleashes

| Take the initiative |

tremendous power. John 15:7 says that "ye shall ask what ye will, and it shall be done unto you" (KJV). Nothing is as powerful to your walk with God as his Word sown into the fabric of your life. As the Word dwells within you, you gain the strength and endurance to act as he would have you, not as our culture would have you.

To memorize Scripture, follow the simple and classic advice of the Nike commercial: "Just do it." Open your Bible and search for promises, principles, and praises. Write down one verse a week on an index card and carry it with you for a week. Read it ten or twenty times a day. At the end of the week, you'll have mastered that verse, and by the end of the year, you'll have stashed away fifty-two nuggets of wisdom.

A second important strategy is to personalize Scripture. Insert your name into favorite Bible passages, along with the words *I*, *me*, and *mine*. This helps you see the Bible as a collection of God's personalized letters, written specifically to you. He's made promises of his faithfulness for every problem, need, circumstance, fear, and frustration. His Word comes alive when you claim it as written specifically to *you*.

For example, 2 Peter 1:3–4 would read:

God's divine power has given me, Tommy, everything I need for life and godliness through our knowledge of him who called me by his own glory and goodness. Through these he has given me his very great and precious promises, so that through them I may participate in the divine nature and escape the corruption in the world caused by evil desires.

John 10:10 would read, "Christ has come so that I, Tommy Newberry, might have life and have it more abundantly."

Put yourself into the pages of the Bible and take ownership of the abundance of spiritual gems that God has laid out for you. It will help you experience the rich, spiritual life people often hope for but typically lack because they fail to recognize the need for discipline in the implementation of truth.

Never underestimate the power of memorizing Scripture, son. This simple discipline holds the key to intimacy with God.

Dad

19

WRITE IT DOWN, MAKE IT HAPPEN

Dear Ty,

There are two ways to shop for groceries. The first is with a list and the second is without. Believe it or not, shopping at our local Publix has many similarities to what the rest of your life will be like. Like life, grocery stores are jam-packed with many things we want and need along with many things we don't want and really do not need. Sometimes these opposing items are even displayed right next to each other, awaiting our selection.

When you head to the supermarket with a shopping list, you increase the chances that you walk out the door with what you want and need. This is common sense. If you skip the list, you will probably check out with some of the things you wanted to buy along with a few extras that you don't really need. No big deal, right? However, when you get home and unpack the bags, you or a close family member is likely to point out something that was forgotten (maybe the TP). This is what commonly happens when you try to keep a list in your head in a world full of distractions and temptations.

I am sure you've figured out that grocery stores try to promote the products they most want to sell. There is, of course, nothing wrong with this. These special items will either be on sale or placed in a spot where we can't miss them or both. Just guessing, but it seems these promotional items are designed for the majority of shoppers who do not bother to use a grocery list. I don't know the exact percentage, but it seems like most people I observe in the grocery store are simply wandering around, simultaneously intrigued and overwhelmed with all the choices at their fingertips.

As you move through the rest of your life, it will be even easier to become overwhelmed with all the fascinating options before you. You are going to be exposed to the heavily promoted values, beliefs, and agendas the culture offers you and wants you to buy (or buy into). You will also be influenced by your mom and me, your faith, your friends and their ambitions, your role models, and maybe even the trends of the day.

Without your own tailor-made shopping list, you are at great risk of getting distracted and arriving at the end of high school, college, or even the end of your life and suddenly realizing that you "forgot" some of the wonderful and important things you intended to accomplish and experience. This happens to millions of people every year, most of whom entered the grocery store of life with good intentions but without a clear list of what they really wanted. I do not want this to be your path.

> Look for the hidden gift 2day

You only get one shot at life, son. My hope for you is that you will strive to live the particular life that God gave you. I don't want you to relive my life. I don't want you to live your sister's life. (That would be really weird.) I want you, instead, to follow your dreams and use your strengths to make a difference in the world in a way that will be divinely purposeful and meaningful and fun. But to live your dreams, you need to define what those dreams looks like. To ensure this happens, I want you to write them down. If you can't or won't write them down, it might still happen for you, but don't count on it.

If you choose to become goal-directed, though, you will enjoy far greater satisfaction and fulfillment as you accomplish the right things year after year after year. Most grown-ups want a better life than what they currently have, but very few have invested the time to figure out exactly what they're really looking for. Generally, they're longing for greater energy, closer relationships, deeper faith, additional income, and more free time. Some want to go on great adventures, while others want to champion great causes. The possibilities are endless, but for the vast majority, they will likely remain only possibilities.

Unfortunately, for most, their vague desires will remain in the distance, not yet out of sight but likely already out of reach. If hopes and dreams remain hidden away in your mind, sharing space with thousands of cluttered and trivial thoughts that bounce around daily and consume your attention, your objectives are likely to remain indefinitely stuck with the status of "someday."

It is easy to become goal directed. And it is also easy to become goal distracted. It is just another life choice and life skill. To become goal directed, convert your broad desires into specifically worded goals that have deadlines and can be easily measured by you or someone else. The more you practice writing your goals or typing them into a digital document, the easier it will become. While many become interested in goals, only a handful become committed to reaching them.

This magnificent minority develops the skill of setting, evaluating, pursuing, tweaking, and assessing their goals. The skills required to become a goal setter can be learned, and anyone can become an expert—including you, son. There are many helpful books and courses that will lead you step-by-step through this process. So learn as much as you can as early as you can. People who become goal setters are better equipped to excel in every area of life they undertake, from mountain climbing and scuba diving to marketing, sales, and marriage.

Planning and goal setting accomplish a number of important objectives. First, goal setting forces you to establish priorities, and in the process, sift through your values as you weigh and measure the most influential factors in your life. Second, as you learn to choose between the good and the best, it will help clear a path before you and help you see where to place your steps. And finally, it will help you create the momentum to bring others with you as you build positive relationships with other people.

Goal setting also produces a chain reaction of positive benefits. Distractions diminish because your course is set. Your motivation will increase as you experience an exciting sense of control over the direction of your life. Because you're thinking back from the future, decision making simplifies, clarifying when to say yes when to say, "No way."

But sometimes life will come at you hard, and you'll get caught in the crossfire of disappointment and pain. But goal setting helps you deal with the hard places in life as well. Goal setters attack problems before those problems have the opportunity to grow and multiply. They create plans, put them in place, then evaluate and reevaluate them, always looking for the opportunity to learn.

When you were small, son, you expressed dreams about what you wanted to be when you became an adult. The reality of life is that you will never accomplish those dreams without putting feet to your goals or boots on the ground, as they say in the military. You have to get out of bed in the morning. Go to school. Take those awful exams. Learn to navigate the adult world of laws, government, and responsibility. Find a way to support yourself.

And the more successfully you can create goals that help you achieve your objectives along the way, the more likely you are to hit your main target. Your enemy will always be complacency. Nothing is more dangerous to your future than assuming you're better than you are or that your skills or your smarts will carry you to success.

Setting goals will help you understand the need to get up earlier and study harder. They will help you understand the importance of working more than the next guy and caring more than you're required to care. They will help you understand that nothing that is worth anything should come easily.

Too many young people today are busy working hard, but they don't seem to be headed anywhere in particular. Most haven't taken the time to think through a life purpose or their goals. Their choices are a series of reactions to parents, circumstances, culture, and friends. But goal-directed young men have the advantage of a built-in navigation system providing turn-by-turn instructions leading directly to their destinations.

Whatever it is you really want, write it down and then make it happen! As my friend Bill Orender encourages others, "Do today what others won't so you can have tomorrow what others can't."[1]

Go for it!

Love,
Dad

20

TRAVEL THE EXTRA MILE

Dear Ty,

On a recent business trip to Miami, I left my iPhone in the car when I was dropped off at the hotel. I didn't realize my phone was missing until about fifteen or twenty minutes later when I was unpacking in my room. Not knowing where I left it, I called the front desk and then the car service.

The car company was very much disinterested in helping me and advised me that the driver wouldn't be available to even look for my phone for at least an hour. I thanked them and hung up the phone. Two minutes later the phone rang in my room. It was the concierge calling to let me know that he would oversee recovering my phone, and he assured me he would get it back to me before midnight.

Then, before he hung up, he said, "You're in Miami. You don't need to worry about your phone. I'll handle it. You relax." Less than forty-five minutes later, and well before midnight, the phone was hand delivered to my room.

Clearly the concierge understands the principle of going the second mile. He did far more than I expected and very likely far more than he was paid to do by his employer. He took the initiative in calling me and not only reassuring me the phone would be located and returned but also that I should just chill and let him do his work. Then he overdelivered by getting my phone back in my hands almost an hour before he promised. He didn't care about being noticed, and he wasn't seeking a tip. He served me in exceptional fashion for the joy of it.

The founder of Wal-Mart, Sam Walton, advised, "Exceed your customer's expectations. If you do, they'll come back over and over. Give them what they want—and a little more. Let them know you appreciate them. Make good on all your mistakes, and don't make excuses—apologize. Stand behind everything you do."[1] The great personal-success advocate Napoleon Hill wrote, "In every soul there has been deposited the seed of a great future, but that seed will never germinate, much less grow to maturity, except through the rendering of useful service."[2]

> Give it your best 2day

To be extraordinary, you have to give something extra to the world. This spirit is captured in a great saying: "If a man only does what is required of him, he is a slave—the moment he begins to do more than he is required, he becomes a free man." When you travel beyond the initial mile, your potential becomes unlimited.

Ty, my desire is for you to be exceptional—not so I can be a proud dad (which I am), but because God is the author of exceptionalism. He calls you to the extraordinary. But in order to be exceptional, you must be willing to go above and beyond, to give more, try more, and prepare more than the rest of the world, and be willing to be measured by a higher standard. But when you learn to take pleasure in doing more than what is expected, your motivation shifts, freeing you to excel and become exceptional.

I encourage you to continuously look for opportunities to exceed expectations. If you are competing in athletics, then out-work and out-hustle your competition. Study the playbook as if your life depended on it. Stay after practice. Get in more reps. Lift a little more. Push yourself more than the coach requires. To reach your maximum, you cannot do the minimum.

Whether part-time or full-time, summer job or permanent position, when you are working, always do more than your boss demands and more than the customers expect. In the business world, doing more than you're paid for is the fastest way to be recognized by bosses, be seen as valuable, get paid more for what you do, and rise to the top as an exceptional employee.

Going the second mile, doing more than the minimum, is a powerful habit for academic achievement, athletic excellence, business success, career advancement, relationship satisfaction, and every other area of your life.

An open door of opportunity awaits you with each new day, Ty. Learn to look for moments to shine—to go the extra mile, to invest in others, and to become exceptional. You're never too young to go the extra mile. Look for ways to double and triple your efforts for the pure joy of it, and watch as God brings honor to his kingdom.

Love you,
Dad

21

DEVELOP YOUR CONFIDENCE

Mason,

Throughout my life, I've observed many very talented individuals who never quite crossed the finish line or delivered their uniqueness to the world simply because they lacked one missing ingredient: confidence. Succinctly stated, confidence is your belief in yourself and your capability to reach the goals that are important to you.

Fortunately, no one is born confident; rather, confidence is a learned habit of mind. Sure, you will meet people who appear to be more naturally confident, but it's no big deal that you may have to occasionally work harder in some areas of life than your peers or competitors. This includes working to gain self-confidence. If you are not as confident as you would like to be, you can become more confident by improving the way you think. Confidence is not an elective life skill; it is required if you want to get the most out of yourself and the most out of your one shot at life.

When you possess confidence, winning and succeeding is much easier. When you lack it, achieving the things you want can seem like pure agony. I've had times in my life when I enjoyed lots of confidence and I've had plenty of seasons where my confidence tank seemed pretty empty. Not surprisingly, the confident periods of my life have produced the greatest progress.

But I want you to understand that I did not accomplish a goal and become confident. Instead, I became confident and accomplished my goal. This is an essential distinction that I hope sinks deeply into your mind.

I do not fully comprehend the power of self-confidence, but I don't need to understand it to appreciate it and put it to good use, and neither do you. Confidence animates, energizes, and multiplies your positive qualities. Explained as a formula, your natural talent multiplied by your confidence equals your full potential. If you have a good sense of humor, confidence will make you even funnier and more entertaining. If you are good at baseball, confidence will make you great. If you are good at cooking, confidence will make you even better. If you are great in math, confidence will take you to the next level. If the girls like you a little bit, with confidence they will like you a lot. It's just another part of the mystery!

You and I have talked about the importance of confidence many times. Without confidence, your growth and development will be stunted. Your talent will lie dormant, buried and unnoticed by others. Lack of confidence is the classic problem of underachievers, those individuals are who blessed with much but deliver very little. Make no mistake; confidence can make the difference between being ordinary and being extraordinary. Regardless of the endeavors you may pursue, confidence will be an essential prerequisite for maximizing your full potential.

Projecting confidence allows you to see and experience an entirely different world than your equally gifted peers who lack this intangible but palpable life enhancer. As a confident young man, you will envision greater possibilities and pursue bigger goals. With lots of confidence, you will be willing to take smart risks, play offense, and face rejection head-on. This gives you an enormous advantage. With confidence you will feel blessed and fortunate, while your buddies lacking confidence will tend to feel unlucky and slighted.

As you go through life, Mason, you will experience both victory and defeat. How you choose to process these moments will sculpt your mind-set and produce confidence or dependency that will, in turn, create positive or negative ripples throughout your life. Confidence helps you think independently, enjoy healthier relationships, deflect peer pressure, and stand firm on your values.

To develop your confidence, first resolve to do so. Then prepare more and work harder than anyone else. Never be outworked. Nothing breeds confidence like knowing you've done your homework and paid the price of success, in full and in advance. Next, begin acting as though you are already the successful person you intend to be, whatever your ambition may be. Practice thinking, talking, acting, and especially feeling as you would if you had already hit your biggest goal.

Accomplishments alone, though, rarely produce lasting confidence. For example, one baseball player goes three for four, but loses confidence because he dwells on the one plate appearance he didn't perform rather than the three he did. Interestingly, another player goes one for four and gains confidence because he replays that one hit over and over again in his head. This scenario repeats itself not just in sports but in all walks of life.

It is worth mentioning that cockiness and conceit are never outgrowths of true confidence but rather counterfeits that reflect an individual's attempt to compensate for insecurity and low confidence. Unfortunately, many Christians smother their confidence to avoid a label of conceit. Consequently, they run the risk of forfeiting their potential as well. Remember, son, virtuous confidence is always accompanied by both gratitude and humility.

True self-confidence grows from appreciating the character of your Creator, from exhaustive preparation, from positive memories, and from a focus on incremental progress instead of perfection. I had you affirm the source of your confidence over and over throughout your childhood: "I am confident in myself because I am confident in my Creator." I know you remember.

Love,
Dad

22

LEVERAGE YOUR STRENGTHS

Dear Mason,

Few things can be as counterproductive in life as investing lots of time doing the wrong things. While this seems like common sense, it is hardly common practice.

Albert Einstein quipped, "Everybody is a genius. But if you judge a fish by its ability to climb a tree, it will live its whole life believing that it is stupid."[1] Similarly, in their classic book *Soar with Your Strengths*, authors Donald Clifton and Paula Nelson share a fable about "Animal School" highlighting a rabbit who is forced by his teachers to spend more time swimming since he is already good at running. In fact, the teacher even arranges for the rabbit to skip running class and have two periods of swimming instead.

> Think about ur goals!

Can you relate to this?

As you know from your school experience, some of your classmates are naturally good at English while others are naturally good at science or math. Of course, most educators want you to be good at everything. Lots of parents want this for their children as well.

Since you are really good in math, Mason, but not so good in English, you have been "asked" plenty of times to stay after school and work on English. If you didn't know better, after years of schooling, it would be easy for you to absorb the message that the key to a successful life is through weakness fixing. If you follow this advice and strive to become less weak at your weaknesses, you will simultaneously become weaker at your strengths. This is a plan I hope you will not follow. Don't be so concerned about becoming well-rounded that you don't develop your own distinct edges. Know what you're good at and become even better at doing it. This strategy can provide you with an invaluable advantage for the rest of your life.

As we've talked about many times, virtually all world-class athletes follow the strengths principle. This means they emphasize the best parts of their game more than the worst parts. Likewise, most great golfers invest their practice time reinforcing their strengths, not repairing their weaknesses. If a specific weakness, such as hitting out of the sand trap, might cost them the tournament, they address it to a minimum level. But they know that champions are created from strength building, not from weakness fixing. Of course, Mason, if you were a seven-year-old boy and haven't yet learned to read, but happened to be a really fast runner, your reading weakness would likely still cost you the "tournament". Obviously, the point I want you to take away is not to ignore your weaknesses altogether but rather to emphasize your strengths.

It is a pretty remarkable achievement to become a straight-A student. I am especially impressed when I see a young person who earns all As while simultaneously participating in sports and other extracurricular activities. I've yet to meet a straight-A grown-up, however (at least one I like), and this point is worth remembering.

You may not be cut out to do it all and be great at lots of things. But this fact should never diminish the effort to identify and develop your area of greatness. I believe everyone has this potential, and you are no exception.

Mason, I want you to be an original masterpiece! You can achieve this by discovering your strengths and putting them into practice to accomplish your goals and God's will for your life. Remember, it is no accident that you are really good at some things and not so good at other things. The same is true for everyone else. God made you extraordinary at certain stuff for a reason. He infused your DNA at creation with particular talent because those gifts line up with his plans for your life. You are also ordinary at a lot of things as well. Get used to it. Be glad for it. It's part of God's plan. And the ordinary list will always be longer than the extraordinary list because there are far too many areas of opportunity, and there are lots of other people in this world who are really extraordinary in the areas where you are only ordinary. If you spend a lot of time on the ordinary stuff, you will sacrifice a bunch of your potential.

This is all part of God's plan. Think about it. If you were exceptional at everything, there would be lots of unnecessary people just hanging out, clogging up the highways and taking up bandwidth. Many of your current peers and future competitors will water down their own potential by doing too many things that God created other people to do. This is a mistake you do not need to make.

Here's the cool thing: since God made us as relational beings, he designed us for collaboration. He created billions of people to partner with him to accomplish his plan for the world. I don't understand exactly how this works, but I know he gives us roles and missions to fulfill on the tight deadline we call our lifetimes.

His purpose for your life coincides with your gifts and talents, and when you pursue your God-implanted mission, you can be sure that the mission God has for your life coincides with your gifts, talents, and passions. Your areas of interest, the activities and pursuits you find most enjoyable, energizing, and attractive, are the best clues to strong talent and giftedness.

When you engage in activities that require your special talent, your brain releases endorphins that trigger within you a sense of satisfaction, joy, and significance as an incentive for you to keep up the good work. As I've shared with you when you asked for help with algebra, I never really experienced these endorphins in math. But I did with baseball and later with coaching and writing. This strong and encouraging sense of satisfaction is a positive reinforcement mechanism that is all part of God's perfect design.

If you practice and stay the course long enough, your talents will eventually get converted into strengths. Unsurprisingly, you will really enjoy operating in your area of strength. Consequently, you will practice and participate over and over again because it makes you feel so good. Once you are out of school, you'll have roughly half of your waking hours devoted to your work life. Therefore, I encourage you to both develop your strengths and follow your passion.

You've lived long enough already to notice that some people are really good at sports and others at singing or painting or designing amazing marketing campaigns. Everyone has an area to shine, but few recognize or cultivate this brilliance because they are too preoccupied at being good at lots of things.

Your one-of-a-kind bundle of character, talents, life experiences, and personality will fuse together and trigger a vision or dream within you. The more often you engage in your strengths, the clearer your ultimate vision will become and the greater things God can do through you. With your God-given talents transformed into strengths, you will become self-motivated, needing less and less prodding from the outside. And this repetitive practice produces champions capable of making giant contributions in the world.

I'm betting that you become one of them!

I love you!

Dad

23

HANG WITH THE WISE

Dear Mason,

Do you remember the old story about the crabs in a bucket? If you put a bunch of crabs in a bucket and watch them, you will see that they will begin to crawl on top of each other to get out of the bucket and back to the beach. They begin to crawl up the side of the bucket. As one of the crabs almost succeeds with his escape, he gets pulled back down into the bucket by his crab friends. The other crabs reach up, grab his leg, and pull him back down into the bucket with them. This is what happens with a bunch of crabs, but if you are not aware of what I want to share with you in this letter, it could happen to you as well.

Ok, I know what you're thinking. Barely a day goes by without me reminding you of the power of association, right? Well, years ago one of my coaches alerted me to this dynamic when he asked if I understood the two reasons I should never wrestle with a pig. I said, "No, what are they?" He replied, "First, you'll just get dirty and second, the pig will like it." This is a very uncomfortable truth.

You have watched this happen over the last few years. Friends and classmates change peer groups and then change habits. Like chameleons, their character is colored by the friends they are hanging out with. How they act depends on who they are with at the moment.

The same is true for you. If you hang out for too long with someone who has a different value system, either you will change or he will change. This realization is the reason I am very sensitive to who is influencing you now and in the future.

Relationships have consequences. The people you spend lots of time with influence the choices you make and the actions you take today and tomorrow. In the long run, your friends influence the kind of person you become. Your character is molded by your choice of friends. Like the buttons on an elevator, your friends will either take you up or down. Relationships are never neutral.

Relationships also influence your excellence. If you want to be a high performer, hang around other high performers. Winners tend to hang around with other winners. As Olympic champion Billy Kidd says, "If you want to be at your best, be with the best." Losers tend to hang with losers who whine and marinate in

> I love u forever, always, no matter what!

mediocrity. Birds of a feather definitely flock together. If you hang out with friends who are committed to good grades, then you'll start hitting the books more often or find another group of friends.

If you are hanging with friends who are striving for athletic excellence, then you will start training harder as well. If you hang on a regular basis with people who whine and act like everything is a hassle, then sooner or later you will resemble them. It's highly unlikely that you will even notice this evolution because changes in character happen so gradually.

Friends will rarely punch, kick, and drag you off course; if that were the case, you would fight back and protect yourself.

Rather, they nudge you just a little bit, then a little bit more, then a hair more, until you are finally off the stage. When people with different values hang out together, somebody ultimately changes. Watch out for mediocre friends who subtly poison your outlook, exhaust your energy, and chip away at your potential for greatness.

You've watched before as I've shared with teenagers a powerful visual about the importance of choosing friends wisely. I get a volunteer to allow me to try to pull him up on the stage using just one arm. I usually pick someone I am unable to lift with just one arm.

After a few exaggerated tries, I ask the teenager to try to pull me down off the stage using just a pinky finger. Even though in most cases I have a nice weight advantage, I am easily pulled off the stage with the power of one little finger. The young adults are a bit surprised and get the message quickly: in life, it's far easier to be pulled down than lifted up.

Every relationship you have, for the rest of your life, son, will be doing one of those two things—lifting you up or pulling you down. It is so easy to let our friends pick us rather than to assertively choose our friends. It is often easier, especially for teenagers, to gravitate toward those who accept us rather than those who will draw the best out of us.

But you are, in effect, a human sponge soaking up the values, worldviews, beliefs, habits, and even the speech patterns, body language, and mannerisms of the people with whom you associate most often. Your family, friends, teammates, and coworkers can reinforce your commitment to your dreams, or they can ever so gradually nudge you down an alternate path.

Other people have immense power to both distract and inspire. It's your responsibility to evaluate the influence your friends and other relationships are having on your journey through life. If you want to understand yourself better, study the people you spend most of your time with. It is very likely that your performance—academic, athletic, or business—as well as your moral compass will match that of your closest peers.

Are you being sharpened by the right friends? In other words, are the people you are hanging out with heading in any cool directions? Are they seeking academic or athletic scholarships? Have they or are they planning to start a business? Have you noticed anything about them that is unique or different from most everyone else?

Do the people you spend most of your time with push you to be your best? As Paul writes in 1 Corinthians 15:33, "Don't be fooled . . . 'bad company corrupts good character'" (NLT). In Proverbs 27:17, we are reminded that one person sharpens another just as iron sharpens iron.

So, if you hang around people who cuss, you will eventually start cussing. If you hang around people who are passionate about the Lord, your faith will grow. If you hang around guys who compromise their integrity, then you are likely to, at some point, do the same thing.

As you spend time reading the Bible, your faith and integrity will increase. Your ability to choose good friends will grow. Your wisdom and discernment will expand. And you will grow in grace and hope (Rom. 15:4 CEV). As George Washington said, "Associate with men of good quality if you esteem your own reputation; for it is better to be alone than in bad company."[1]

This is my prayer for you, son: associate with the wise and become wise. Become an influence for godliness upon others. Become the man of God you were created to be and who you are already becoming.

Love,
Dad

24

REFLECT TRUE AMERICAN CHARACTER

Dear Trey,

America's distinctive character flows from the wisdom of the Founding Fathers and the blessings of the heavenly Father, who inspired them. In spite of our imperfections, America has demonstrated exceptional moral strength from its founding. As with individuals, a country's character is revealed when it is under fire. When an individual or a country is tested, the world finds out what they're really made of. Time and time again, when America has been tested, the red, white, and blue fibers of virtue have been crisply and proudly illuminated.

For example, Todd Beamer, Jeremy Glick, and the other heroes of United Airlines Flight 93 revealed their character, and by extension, the nation's character, when they were unexpectedly drafted into battle on the morning of September 11, 2001. Aware of the fate of the other hijacked planes, these martyrs counterattacked against the Islamic terrorists who intended to use their jetliner as a weapon to kill hundreds or perhaps thousands more Americans. Had these everyday American passengers lacked the courage of character to fight back, either the White House or the Capitol would probably have been destroyed. The bold sacrifice of the Flight 93 heroes is a powerful reminder of the role individual citizens play in the defense of our freedoms. We have walked our talk more consistently and honorably than any nation on earth.

The Judeo-Christian roots woven through our founding documents are our country's greatest asset. Our character still carries the legacy of godly men who boldly fought for our independence from England and established our republic. Our Founders considered strong religious beliefs to be vital to strong character—from the moral laws of the Ten Commandments to the inalienable rights given us by our Creator. "In God We Trust," which was added to US coins during the Civil War, was not chosen as a political slogan but an expression of the faith of a nation.

> God must have really loved me to give me u

Good character exists within each one of us to the degree that we choose good over evil. More than any other factor, our character is responsible for our achievement or underachievement in life—whether in politics, business, marriage, or sports. As any good football coach reminds his players, "Character is what you're made of." And the character of a nation is made up of the sum of its virtuous citizens. America's character is America's backbone.

A couple of years ago, while I was hanging out at the beach with friends, we began complaining about America's real and supposed problems. A question occurred to me, and I posed it to everyone, "If America isn't the greatest nation that exists, which nation is, and why aren't we living there?"

No one had an answer.

It's not an accident that immigrants have streamed into America for over two hundred years: it's the greatest land of opportunity ever founded. Regardless of your heritage, this is the place where you have a shot at designing your life and making your dreams come true. In America, your life can become an example for others to follow or a warning for others to heed. You can be born poor and earn a fortune, be born rich and lose it all, or live life somewhere in the middle. It's up to you. What a country!

American patriotism fades in and out of fashion, especially in certain intellectual circles. But I'll say it straight: America is the best of the best.

Beginning with the bravery of our Founders and their fight for freedom, through numerous wars, the Great Depression, and the attacks of September 11, we have fought back from adversity. And we have what it takes to make yet another comeback.

America is an exceptional country. It is different from all others because our people are different—our national character has been shaped by our unique values and by the circumstances of our nation's founding through our fight for liberty. Without apology, we claim a unique destiny. We're something special. Theodore Roosevelt stated, "There can be no divided allegiance here. Any man who says he is an American, but something else also, isn't an American at all."[1]

America is a unique country with a distinct national character and an unmatched way of life. Those things are worth fighting for, son. I pray that you will.

Love,

Dad

25

BUILD PRODUCTIVE HABITS

Brooks,

Your grandfather once told me that he attributed much of his success to simply developing worthwhile habits. He said, "I just got into the habit of consistently doing the productive thing most of the time, and I maintained that habit over several decades."

Habits are nothing more than behaviors that have become automatic through repetition and affirmation. Please remember that every habit, whether helpful or hurtful, adds color and definition to your character. Some of your habits revolve around your goals while others spring up out of fear. Constructive habits produce positive results and conserve willpower for other endeavors. Destructive habits become enemies of your potential, attempting to rob you of God's great plans.

Up to this point, you have unknowingly or deliberately ingrained spiritual habits, emotional habits, mental habits, physical habits, and financial habits. Some of your habits strengthen your relationship with God; some do not. Some of your habits help you earn better grades; some do not. Some of your habits make you a more competitive athlete; some do not. Some of your habits make you a better friend; some do not. Some of your

God is good!

habits make you a better steward of your time and talent; some do not.

Author and leadership coach Steven Covey wrote, "Our character is basically a composite of our habits. Because they are consistent, often unconscious patterns, they constantly, daily, express our character."[1] And one of the founders of our great nation, Ben Franklin, noted, "Each year one vicious habit rooted out, in time might make the worst man good throughout."[2] Incidentally, I would recommend that you read as much as you can from what both Covey and Franklin have written.

At this very moment, you possess both productive and unproductive habits. This is true for all of us. Some of your habits are specific and precise, such as doing two hundred pushups every day, memorizing a Bible verse each week, or brushing your teeth two or three times a day. Other habits are broad, such as treating others well, eating healthy, or going the second mile. But all habits have one thing in common: they either move you toward the person God created you to be or they move you away. Each habit either develops or weakens your character.

As you go through life, I urge you to pay attention to your habits. From time to time, make an inventory of the things you consistently do in your life whether positive or negative. Then connect each habit you identify to a goal you have or a character quality you are striving to possess. Be brutally honest with yourself.

Then resolve to replace a weak habit with an excellent habit. I've found it's best to work on one habit at a time. This way you won't get overwhelmed or discouraged. Besides, there is usually no need to rush. At your age, you are building a foundation with many of your habits that will follow you for a lifetime. Build one better habit until it has taken root and become an automatic extension of who you are. In about thirty uninterrupted days, you can lock in a new habit. (It might take ninety days if you have a few misses here and there.)

When it comes to your habits, you will either be their master or their slave.

Dad

26

STAY AWAY FROM PORN

Zach,

I'd be leaving out an important message if I didn't talk to you about porn. Pornography has been around for a long time. When I was growing up, it seemed to be limited to magazines and the shady area of town. A lot has changed. Today, thanks to the digital revolution and the anonymity it provides, porn is virtually everywhere.

The ugly truth is that more than 50 percent of men, including Christian men, of all ages today struggle with porn.[1] This includes the men, teens, and even young boys we rub elbows with in our churches, | I believe in u! | classrooms, business meetings, and sporting events every day—even pastors. More recently, pornography has spread to women as well. I don't need to tell you that porn is accessible to everyone. You know what kids are downloading on their phones and laptops these days.

Porn isn't just somebody else's problem, though. It's ours because it has saturated our culture. As men, we're called to take a stand for our families and our nation, and to defend the dignity of women. By the time you're a father, son, porn may have done irreversible damage to our nation's moral fiber and the sanctity of our families.

You should be aware that growing numbers of Christians

have convinced themselves that using porn is acceptable or okay in certain circumstances. Like all men, Christian men can be tempted in moments of loneliness or anger to turn to pornography as a substitute for authentic sexual expression the way God intended.

We are called to love the things God loves and hate the things he hates. Pornography is an assault against the integrity of women. Every woman is somebody's daughter or sister, but first and foremost a daughter of God, and second, the daughter of a mother who gave birth to her and parents who raised her. Porn reduces her to an object or commodity, something to be used and discarded.

Everywhere you look, everywhere you walk, porn calls out to you. Temptation is only a glance or a click away. If you haven't been disciplined in how to respond, how to walk away, how to guard your mind and your eyes, you're as likely as the next guy to be surfing the Net or downloading games or videos on your iPhone or iPod when explicit images hijack and then preoccupy your attention.

And addiction can cling to you for a lifetime. Of course, not everyone exposed to porn becomes addicted to it. But the companies that produce porn certainly hope you will. And they have male biology on their side. An addicted customer keeps coming back for more. And so they fill their porn with images that get the hormones flowing. No need to inhale or shoot up any drug with a needle to get addicted to porn; your body will make its own drugs just by viewing the images. Studies show that using porn literally changes the chemistry of the brain.

Some will just come away with toxic ideas about women, sex, and marriage. That kind of damage is bad enough. But porn isn't the only ingredient in this kind of addiction. Usually, those who become addicted have some kind of spiritual or emotional void that allows the attraction to really take root and become addictive.

Porn is a trap. It tempts you with promises of fulfillment and mires you in guilt, shame, and deception. Porn weakens your opportunity to have an authentic, honest relationship with a woman, the way God intended.

Don't sell yourself short and accept second best—for yourself or the woman you may one day love.

Love,
Dad

27

RECOGNIZE TRUTH

Dear Zach,

You're living at a unique time in history when long-held beliefs are being questioned. Frankly, Zach, you're living in a truth war. When you head off to college, this will become even more obvious to you. We've talked about it, and you've seen the battle lines drawn during your lifetime. Relativism is the new standard of truth. This means that what has been black and white for generations has faded into multiple shades of gray. In this relative worldview, no principle, religion, nation, or position is superior to another.

For this reason, it is essential that you have the capability to distinguish between truth and fiction. If you are not clear about what is true and right, it will be hard for you to spot what can be very clever counterfeits. And this isn't just true of political or social positions. It's also become true within the church. A movement is sweeping the nation that questions whether Christians can ever truly understand the message of the gospel. Leaders of this movement admit that God spoke through the Bible but say that the true intent of his message can't be known.

This leaves us as God followers in a pretty interesting position. Our commander in chief supposedly left us with a battle plan—the Bible—that he never intended for us to really figure out. And if we can't figure out his message, we can't be held responsible for following it or sharing it with the world. We're pretty much left on our own to apply our own assumptions to what the Bible means.

At its simplest level, this logic doesn't make sense. The God of the universe chose to communicate with us—not to confuse us or leave us puzzled, but so we could know him and his plan for humanity. But before we can hear his voice, we have to invite him into our lives. He knew that without his truth as a foundation for life, his children would build egocentric societies on the sinking sands of secularism and relativism. And so he provided truth through his Son, the living Word, and truth through the Bible, the written Word.

> U r going to be so successful!

Truth is taking a beating in this day and age, Zach. But you will always be able to recognize the truth by laying it side by side against Scripture. Now, more than ever, it is important for you, first of all, to *know the Word of God*—not just what it says on the surface or what it says here and there, but to know how to dig deep for truth. Become a student of the Bible. Get involved in a church that teaches Scripture, and plug into men's groups, accountability groups, and Bible studies.

Second, you need to make yourself accountable to the people of God. It can be easy for us to twist truth to fit our circumstances when life becomes challenging. That's where godly friends will play an important role in keeping you grounded. Find accountability partners who will hold your feet to the fire. Talk about the tough stuff, and don't be afraid to let them challenge you.

Third, listen for the leading and conviction of the Spirit of God. You'll be tempted at times to compromise on truth—in your job, in your relationships, in secret places you don't think people will know about. In the years ahead, it will become harder to take a stand on what the Bible says. Be sensitive to the Spirit of God. Really listen. Then act on what you hear. Your decisions will shape your future for the rest of your life. Through the power of the Holy Spirit, God's Word *will* speak to you.

"I write these things to you who believe in the name of the Son of God so that you may know that you have eternal life" (1 John 5:13 NIV). God wrote to us so we might *know*. Not guess about what he had in mind. His truth doesn't change.

You can stake your life on it and never be disappointed.

Love,
Dad

28

PRAYER IS ALWAYS THE ANSWER

Dear Ty,

When I was young, something inside me secretly wanted to believe that the tragedies of life would never come my way. I didn't want to think my future might include loved ones dying or being diagnosed with nasty illnesses or that my house could one day burn down.

But I grew up, of course, and learned that the pain of life hits all of us. We live in a broken world filled with broken people. Sooner or later, Ty, you'll hit a brick wall of crisis that will send you skidding through the dirt, and the experience won't be fun. It's at these moments in life that most people ask for prayer.

Here's what I want you to remember: God loves us so much that he never wants to be even a breath away from us. He has hardwired us to himself through our self-talk and the power of prayer. It breaks his heart that we often just show up for help in the tough times when he created us so he could hang out and have a relationship with us.

I encourage you to make prayer the highest calling of your life, son. It gives you contact to the God of the universe 24-7 and provides power for everything you will ever hope to accomplish. It's your line of access to a relationship with God. The instant you pray, something in you or about you is altered for the better. Prayer changes things. Most definitely, prayer changes your character for the better. Prayer is not just a way to bring your wish list to God or to tune up your spiritual life. Believe in your prayers. They are the source and strength of your spiritual life.

Prayer is the answer when life seems good, and you need to be reminded you're not the boss and you're dependent on God for everything. Prayer is the answer when friends fail you and you need to know that Jesus never leaves your side—no matter what. Prayer is the answer when you feel miserable or terrified but don't have anyone nearby you can trust. Prayer is the answer when you need to be reassured that God knows the beginning and the end, no matter what you see at the moment.

> U have what it takes!

Prayer is also the answer when you've gotten the promotion or the raise or won the championship, and you're tempted to think you're good enough or strong enough to do life on your own. Prayer is the answer when you don't have words at all and the Holy Spirit speaks for you, saying all you will ever need and more to the Father.

Prayer is just communication between you and God. This means it includes listening as well as talking or asking. Remember, he is the vine and we are the branches. If you're a branch, very little good can ever come if you are cut off from the vine, right? To experience his presence and power you must stay connected to him. It is your responsibility to initiate and maintain this life link despite your busy schedule. You can accomplish this through continuous conversation and confession.

God is a real and vivid force in your life, always present and available to be contacted through our very thoughts. He's never more than a thought away. Instead of keeping prayer for bedtime or before meals and important events, pray continuously throughout the day. These prayers can be casual and conversational, as though you were chatting with me, with a buddy, or with one of your uncles. The main priority is to come clean about your sins right away. Own up to your poor decisions immediately, especially those choices you knew were wrong before you made them. Never let sins, frustrations, or disappointments accumulate. Hand off both your blunders and burdens to Jesus ASAP.

Next, ask the Lord for help all day long. Ask for his ideas. Ask for his feedback. Seek his direction on both the easy stuff and difficult challenges of the day. Maybe it is the day before final exams. Pray. Maybe it is an hour before the state championship. Pray. Maybe it is the moment before you break up with your girlfriend or the moment after she dumps you. Pray. Maybe it is when you first hear that a friend you've known since kindergarten has just been killed in a car wreck. Pray. Maybe it is when you just got caught doing something you know is wrong. Pray. Maybe it is the second you learn of a catastrophe across the world from where you stand. Pray. Maybe it is the minute before you leave your apartment for a day at the beach with friends. Pray.

Confused after an argument with your professor? Ask God for wisdom. Don't feel like studying? Ask him for self-discipline. Disturbed after watching the national news? Ask him how you could be part of the solution. He is never too busy to help you navigate life's challenges or celebrate its victories either. Prayer is always the answer.

Since you were very young, we have prayed together daily, almost every morning and every night and before all important events and activities. Now I challenge you to take your prayer life to the next level. Whether admitting sin or asking for help,

I hope you'll keep a constant dialog going with the Creator of the universe. Stay plugged into the Almighty. In so doing, you stay connected to eternity while remaining fully alive in each moment.

May God give you a heart to see the power of prayer in your life, Ty, and to thirst to spend time with him. Walk with God, talk with God, serve God, and love God. And may your joy explode as you spend time with him and see his great and loving heart for you.

Love,
Dad

29

FOCUS ON STEWARDSHIP

Dear Ty,

I remember the first time your mom and I left the house for the evening and trusted you to be in charge of things on the home front. We didn't take the decision lightly. After all, we were entrusting you with the safety of everything we had, including your little brother. And, of course, you shouldered the responsibility just the way we knew you would, and you made us proud.

The word *stewardship* is often misunderstood. A lot of people think stewardship is just about money. But what it really means is that we've been called to be managers of God's household. What's amazing about this is that God didn't just hand us the keys to his house. He expects us and has trusted us to conscientiously take care of the blessings he has provided. This includes personal gifts such as your mind and body, your physical or creative talent, your family, your relationships, your sexuality, your possessions, and your financial resources. It also includes universal blessings such as the environment and our freedom as a nation. Stewardship is the practice of taking care of what we have.

When you accept that God, not you, really owns it all and is but temporarily sharing it with you, it heightens your sense of gratitude for what you do have and encourages you to be both purposeful and generous. It can't help but change your perspective when you realize God created you to be in charge of his stuff. He also created you to be an owner. He gave you the ability to earn and to accumulate wealth so you could influence the world.

Think about it. God wants to partner with *you* to work out his plan for the universe. Wrap your mind around that fact, and it will change the way you look at everything. Your iPhone, your love of music, your athletic ability, and your aptitude for technology all have one thing in common: they are all blessings you've been entrusted with and are expected to take care of for God's glory.

As a steward, you're called to be a leader, not one of the crowd. God never divided his world into "secular" and "sacred." To God, all of life is spiritual. Look at everything you do as stewardship of his world for his honor. Therefore, your character must be rock solid. On behalf of God, you're responsible to look out for the needs of other people, exhibit faith-driven joy, and above all, share God's passions—to love the things he loves and hate the things he hates. Listen for his heartbeat, son, and make it the pulse that drives your own life.

> I believe something wonderful is happening 2 u today!

The parable of the talents in Matthew 25 highlights the demands and rewards of stewardship. It's not enough for you to appreciate the gifts God gives you or even to use them. God expects you to invest each and every good gift, whether it's a skill for cooking or an ability to toss an accurate fifty-yard pass.

An understanding of stewardship also reinforces the importance of merit over equality. In the parable of the talents, the master gave his servants different amounts of money according to their differing abilities to handle money. Everyone did not receive equally because everyone was not able to manage equally. The parable also teaches the importance of stewardship. The master was pleased when the first two servants invested his money and angry when the third simply hid his money away. The parable also teaches one more important lesson about stewardship: good stewards aren't excuse-making victims. The third servant pointed his finger at his master and suggested he was unfair, greedy, and corrupt, then blamed his bad decision on fear of his master. But the master was a wise steward. He didn't buckle under the emotional pressure.

Instead, he gave the servant's single talent to the most successful servant who'd earned ten and heaved the "worthless slave" into outer darkness. The lesson is obvious: God isn't as interested in what we have as much as he's interested in what we make of what we have, whether we multiply it or diminish it. The old Boy Scout rule is to leave things in as good a condition as you found them. But the parable of the talents goes beyond that, insisting we should make things better than we got them.

So what has God given you, son, and what are you doing to invest those things? God has left you with the keys to his kingdom, and he's counting on you to make him proud.

Love,
Dad

30

TROPHIES AREN'T
FOR EVERYONE

Dear Ty,

I bet you can still remember receiving your first trophy at a pizza restaurant when you were only about six or seven years old. The coach called your name and handed you the trophy as the rest of the team began to enthusiastically laugh when they realized your trophy was mistakenly a "girl soccer trophy." Twenty minutes later, in a fit of good-spirited rage, you "accidentally" broke the trophy on the surface of our driveway when we arrived back home. I couldn't blame you, and I believe that it was pure coincidence that you never played another game of soccer.

That mini-drama created the perfect opportunity to share with you that you really didn't deserve a trophy at all. I said that not because you were really bad but because you were, at soccer, only average. And being average doesn't, or at least shouldn't, merit special attention. I probably conveyed that point more gently at the time, but you got the point anyway and handled the revelation like a man.

Ty, you have grown up during an era of entitlement when most youth sports leagues have tried to make things "fair and equal" by awarding trophies to everyone just for showing up and playing on the team. In reality, they don't even have to show up to get their trophy as long as their parents have paid the registration fee. This seemingly harmless practice got underway sometime during the 1980s with the intention of building the self-esteem of kids. Of course, false recognition only produces counterfeit self-worth at best. Giving someone something he has not earned does not strengthen his self-worth or build anything desirable.

While there is no harm in recognizing participation, a trophy should be reserved for accomplishment, excellence, and demonstrated leadership skills. Its purpose is to motivate not only the deserving recipient but other ambitious athletes who aspire to get the next trophy. Think about it. When trophies are robotically distributed to everybody on the team, those who should be singled out for merit are overlooked, and those who don't deserve recognition receive it just for participating. Do you think society can produce more winners simply by handing out more trophies?

It is important to me that you understand that the trophies-for-everyone mentality does not reflect how the real world works. Rather, it instills the expectation of getting something for nothing and teaches that life rewards participation as much as or even more than results. It suggests that life will always be fair and that it's not particularly important how much or how little you contribute or accomplish.

Game balls—an old tradition in which the top performer in a particular game is given an honorary game ball—work the same way. They reward and inspire. Those are two great words when you put them in the context of rewarding success and inspiring greatness. But again, that's not how game balls are always used anymore. Do you remember the coach I assisted

101

who planned out in advance when each player on his team would be given the game ball? It was nice, I suppose, but by the third or fourth game, the kids had caught on to the well-meaning ruse. I know of retail stores and banks that follow the same program with grown-ups, predetermining the employee of the week a year ahead of time to make sure no one gets overlooked. And the result is the same as for the coach's game balls—an honor loses any meaning when it's given out to everyone.

Youth sports have traditionally been a great venue to develop character through competition, as kids tasted both victory and defeat. By definition, we can't have winners unless we have losers. But sports have been compromised with social agendas and increasingly absorbed into the fairness movement. In an apparent attempt to neutralize the concept of winning and losing, some youth leagues around the nation don't even keep score anymore—even though the kids, of course, still do.

Winning may not be everything, but it is right up there with oxygen. But, by now, you know there is also immense value in losing. For example, I have been a loser far more than I have been a winner (no jokes, please), and every time I lose, it spurs me to work even harder so I don't have to be a loser again the next time around. If every competition had to finish in a tie, it would end competition and quickly become a bore to watch. What would the Olympics be like if every athlete earned a medal? What would Saturday afternoons in the fall be like if the football games ended in a tie?

One Saturday afternoon, when you were helping me clean out and reorganize the attic, you noticed a label that caught your eye. It read "Tommy's Trophies." Excited to possibly verify some of my childhood success stories, you rushed to open the box only to find seven trophies inside. You pointed out that there were *only seven* trophies and asked me where the rest were.

When I told you that was the entire collection, you laughed and didn't believe me. I told you that while there were *only seven*, I had earned them all. We walked downstairs and to your bedroom where there were fifteen or so trophies crowded onto the top of your dresser. It was then that I explained in detail the difference between a participation trophy and an earned or merit-based trophy.

Two or three years later I recall the expression on your face as you crossed the finish line of a school race in second place. After your name was announced on the loud speakers and you posed for a picture, you came directly to me, held the trophy up, and still out of breath, exclaimed, "Dad, I earned this one!" "You sure did," I responded, "and I am very proud of you."

Love,

Dad

31

EARN, GIVE, SAVE, AND SPEND

Dear Trey,

Lack of money can cause all sorts of problems and pain. However, having plenty of money doesn't remove the problems of life either. In truth, money is neutral. It is simply the medium through which people exchange their goods and services. How you learn to think about and manage your money is what really counts. If you think properly about money, then you will be more effective in *earning, giving, saving, investing,* and *spending* it.

As you develop your philosophy about personal finances, these are a few things I want you to keep in mind:

First and foremost, *remember that God owns it all.* I've shared this concept of stewardship with you many times before. God has entrusted you to take care of and multiply your blessings. If you have lots of money, God wants you to do lots of good things with it. For to him who has been given much, much will be expected (Luke 12:48). As reiterated in the parable of the talents, if you have only a little money, God still wants you to use it wisely and generously.

Develop constructive beliefs about money. Money is a fascinating subject to discuss, and it is very important to understand it! Lots of people have hang-ups about money. Some people associate negativity with money. Some people believe money is downright evil, or at least the root of all evil. The Bible actually says that "the love of money is the root of all evil" (1 Tim. 6:10 KJV). Not money itself. Others believe rich people are necessarily greedy, corrupt, or lucky and so on.

I want to assure you that there is nothing wrong with having money in the bank as long as that money doesn't own a big chunk of your heart. If you worship and depend on your affluence more than you depend on God, there is a big problem. But if you are a prudent and generous steward of your money, then your finances can be a real blessing to your family and many others you choose to enrich with your resources. God doesn't care whether you have ten dollars or ten million. He cares where your heart is. He cares what you are living for, what you are devoted to, and what you are depending on.

> What r u looking forward 2?

There is no amount of academic or athletic accomplishment that is sinful. Likewise, there is no amount of financial wealth that is immoral. However, any of these worldly accomplishments could swell your opinion of yourself to the point where you stop looking to God and seek your own reflection instead. That's what you must resist—not wealth. It's not what we have that may separate us from God; rather, it's what has us that really matters.

What you assume about money and wealth will influence your work habits, your earning ability, and how you give, save, invest, and spend. Some people believe profit and wealth are sinful or somehow oppressive to the poor. If so, Scripture would certainly condemn such practice. It does not. The Bible never condemns wealth. To the contrary, Scripture speaks of prosperity as a blessing. Throughout the Bible, God rewards people who are good stewards with wealth and property. For example, when God told Solomon to ask for whatever he wanted, Solomon asked for wisdom. God was so pleased with this unselfish answer that he rewarded him not only with unmatched wisdom but vast riches and honor as well.

God ordains wealth because it provides the opportunity for individual stewardship. And God requires stewardship. Throughout the Scriptures, we are called to be wise and faithful stewards. As you know, stewardship is the practice of taking care of the blessings that are entrusted to us and can refer to taking care of money, physical talent, creative talent, relationships, children, property or physical possessions, and much more.

Practice delayed gratification. One of the best indicators of financial success is the learned ability to delay gratification. Many Americans simply buy something when they feel like buying something whether or not it fits into their budget or they can afford it. By avoiding the black hole of spontaneous, emotion-driven buying, you can become financially responsible and ultimately financially independent far sooner and with much less stress.

When making personal financial decisions, take into consideration the longest time period when making your day-to-day spending decisions. By sacrificing financially in the short term, you will create financial strength in the long term. If you insist on having all your material desires satisfied today, you will be risking long-term financial success tomorrow. Decide how you want to live now versus how long you want to have to work. If you spend most or all of what you earn right now, then you will be obligated to work longer. This will not be a choice, but a necessity. Living more modestly today means you will have a lot more choices tomorrow. Choosing to sacrifice today to preserve a bigger reward tomorrow will be a wise, no-regrets decision that will bless you and your future family. This is the difference between a short-term point of view and a longterm perspective.

Practice immediate gratitude. By deliberately reminding yourself of your current blessings, financial and otherwise, you bring about a mind-set conducive to abundance and wealth creation. Appreciate all the good in your life as well as all the bad that is not in your life. When you give thanks and feel blessed in the current moment, you tend to bring about better moments in the future. When you feel entitled or slighted in the present moment, you tend to bring about more bad stuff to complain about. During difficult stretches, it may be hard to count your blessings, but the simple practice (maybe at bedtime, in the shower, or while commuting) can help you experience true wealth regardless of your current financial status.

Avoid a scarcity mind-set. This is an all-too-common belief that the pie of abundance contains only a fixed number of pieces. Rooted in fear, a scarcity mind-set highlights what is missing or deficient, not what is available or could be available with a little bit of work. To be financially successful, avoid this deep-rooted fear that there is not enough of the good stuff for everyone. Of course, God's creation is not limited or scarce in the least, but if you mistakenly think it is, then for all practical purposes, it will be—for you.

The pie of abundance is not limited. There are an infinite number of pies, and bigger pies are created every time value is created. You can create more value in your home, in your community, and in the world, and this abundance is self-perpetuating. The more you create, the more people are impacted and the more abundance is multiplied.

Establish financial goals. It is important to know where

you are financially so you can design a plan to get where you'd rather be down the road. If you enter a field with great financial opportunity, then aim high. How much should you earn? Earn as much as you can. Our nation and the entire would is in dire need of wealthy Christians who will direct and share the resources with worthy causes around the globe.

But it is essential that you set clear, specific financial goals. It is not enough to want plenty of money or to strive for financial security. You need to commit in writing to exactly how much money you intend to earn, by when, and how you will accumulate it. Pick a date in the future, maybe five or ten years from now, and commit to earning and saving a specific amount of money by that deadline. Most people hope for more money, but only few intensely desire it, and even fewer develop an intelligent goal and strategic plan to make it happen.

Brainstorm regularly about how you can increase your service. The amount of money you earn in a competitive marketplace is the measure of value that others place on your contribution. By the way, it is okay if this gauge stings your ego a little from time to time. Accepting this reality will set you free and kick off a chain reaction of positive progress.

To earn more, become more valuable to others. Realize that success is achieved not at the expense of others but in service to them. Money is a result, not a cause. Therefore, to increase the amount of money you are taking out of the economy, first increase the value of the work you are putting into it. Regardless of your job, whether permanent or part-time, invest a half hour every week to brainstorm ways you could better serve your customers and/or your boss.

Give at least 10 percent of your income to Christ-centered charities. Identify those Christian causes that have a proven track record of faithfully investing and deploying their resources.

Examine closely the values and philosophy of even Christian charities to make sure your money is not going to support causes that violate your values and intentions.

Giving is an important role that all of us are called to joyfully participate in. In the New Testament, we are reminded of the giving principle, that our giving determines our getting. Jesus said, "Give, and it will be given to you. A good measure, pressed down, shaken together and running over, will be poured into your lap. For with the measure you use, it will be measured to you" (Luke 6:38 NIV). In other words, we should give early and give often. Saint Francis of Assisi said, "For it is in giving that we receive."[1] *Save at least 10 percent* of your income in low-risk accounts. Then invest 10 percent of your income in ventures that have the potential to multiply in significant ways. Budget around the remaining 70 percent and adjust your lifestyle accordingly. Discipline yourself to live like this.

Wealth can mean different things to different people. To one person, wealth is having no debt. To others, wealth is being able to live the lifestyle they desire. To others, wealth is having a few million in the bank. The amount of money you will need in order to experience wealth is up to you.

But wealth earned and held by Christians will be wealth shared. With wealth, you can be free of financial pressure, have more opportunities, experience greater freedom in how you live your life, help more causes, and while you are improving the quality of your life, you can improve the quality of many other lives simultaneously.

The time to ingrain productive financial habits is now. If you won't give 10 percent of the dollar you earned from being a camp counselor last summer, then do you really think you will give 10 percent when you have a permanent income? If you will not donate ten bucks when you earn one hundred, then you are kidding yourself if you think you will donate ten thousand when you earn one hundred thousand.

There's a lot you need to learn on you own about money. It can be a great blessing or a perpetual thorn in your side, and your choices will help determine which. I hope what I've written here will give you a head start. If you stick to the proper sequence—earn, give, save, and spend—you'll be well on your way.

Love,
Dad

32

THINK HUGE

Dear Mason,

The British prime minister of the late 1800s, Benjamin Disraeli, once said that "life is too short to be little."[1] What do you think he meant by this? One of my favorite authors, Claude Bristol, put it like this, "You have to think big to be big."[2] The great Chicago architect and city planner Daniel Burnham wrote, "Make no little plans; they have no magic to stir men's blood and probably will themselves not be realized. Make big plans; aim high in hope and work, remembering that a noble, logical diagram once recorded will not die."[3]

One of the most important factors influencing your success in life, if not the most important, is how you choose to think. As we have discussed on many occasions, God has blessed you with a wide range of choices.

You can think positively or negatively. You can think critically or constructively. You can think creatively or conventionally. You can think faithfully or anxiously. You can think selfishly or generously. You can think independently or dependently. And you can think little or you can *think huge*. Keep in mind that the way you consistently think eventually locks in as a habit and steers you into the future much like a jet's autopilot feature. Once your automatic thinking patterns are established, they are difficult to adjust.

You have heard me say the phrase "think huge" over and over again. And it is one of the most frequent commands heard in my coaching center. But what does "think huge" actually mean?

To think huge is to think beyond who you are today to the person you could become tomorrow. Huge thinking is a learned mind-set or attitude possessed by most peak performers. It encompasses several areas of deliberate thought and intention. To think huge is to think more about possibilities than probabilities. It is future-focused thinking dominated not by what is true today but by what could be true tomorrow, next week, next month, next year, or even next decade.

Huge thinking is ambitious thinking rooted

in faith, not fear. Consequently, huge thinkers see opportunities where others see
problems. Huge thinkers approach goal setting
a bit unconventionally, deliberately estab-
lishing goals that they do not yet know how to
achieve. This means setting "game-changer"
and "life-changer" goals that carry with them
the potential to dramatically upgrade their
opportunities.

Not only does this feel awkward and defy
common sense, it also sets them up for possible
failure and even embarrassment. Nonetheless,
a huge thinker does this anyway, knowing it will
pay off in the long run, and quite possibly in
the short term as well. The magnificent minority who bother to set goals at all typically
stumble on the side of pursuing small objectives
that simply tinker around the edges of their
full potential, providing little if any personal
satisfaction or public inspiration to others.
But huge thinkers refuse to settle for good
enough—whether in their schoolwork, athletics, relationships, career aspirations, health, or
personal finances.

Huge thinkers know that there are no
uncreative people, only people with small, dull
goals. This gives them a distinct advantage.

The very act of writing down compelling goals unlocks creative reserves waiting to be tapped into. The catalyst for this dynamic is the simple act of writing and definitely committing to the huge goal. This act kicks off a chain reaction of goal-achieving coincidences that never would have occurred in the absence of the huge goal. By setting huge goals, you'll become a difference maker. Your influence and responsibility will grow, as will your opportunity for impacting others in a positive and permanent way.

The philosopher Henry David Thoreau wrote, "What lies behind us and what lies before us are tiny matters compared to what lies within us."[4] Only when you start thinking huge will those words ring true—and then you'll begin to catch a glimpse of what truly lies within.

Believe it!

Love,
Dad

33

MARRIAGE IS A COVENANT

Dear Ty,

When I was in college, one of my sisters gave me a book titled *Everything Men Know about Women* as my Christmas present. When I opened it, I discovered it was completely blank. Well, I have learned a lot about women, and in particular, marriage, since then. I was even thinking about "writing" my own gag book called *Everything Young Couples Know about Marriage*, and this book would be empty as well.

By the time you decide to get married, I want you to be able to fill up at least a few pages with the insights you have learned from your mom and me and others prior to making that most important commitment.

I know it is sort of weird to ask you to think about getting married when it seems as though that reality is so far in the distance. Nonetheless, time passes quicker than you may now realize, and before you know it, you may be asking that special girl to spend the rest of her life with you.

I want you to know that there are some things that happen when you are single that influence the quality of your relationship once you are married. If you wait to learn about these dynamics until you are about to get married, then it will probably be too late for them to benefit you in any meaningful way.

First, I want you to understand that marriage is a covenant between you, your wife, and God. Your heavenly Father considers marriage to be more than a legal document or a good thing for society. He created marriage as a covenant—a binding relationship meant to last a lifetime. God considers marriage to be holy and a picture of the unity of Jesus and the church. When a man and a woman get married, two people become one and become a living, breathing example of God's nature and character. This is why God uses images of brides and marriage feasts when he talks about his love for us and the church, his people. This is an important paradigm shift compared with what you observe in our culture today, but a perspective that is critical to understand well ahead of time.

What's the wise thing 2 do?

One reason God designed marriage to be this way is that it is humanly impossible for a man and a woman to meet each other's needs by themselves without the help of God. Just consider the complexity of permanently merging together two very different human beings, no strings attached, forever! This explains why today about half of all marriages end in divorce, with all the pain, suffering, and multigenerational consequences that go along with it.

During dating, love is largely an expression of your feelings. Once married, love becomes more of a giving of yourself and an expression of your will, not just your feelings. And sometimes it will be more will than feeling, and this is okay. But neither you nor your future wife is capable of fully meeting the other's needs and expectations. If you and your bride-to-be are not aware of this as single adults, it can come as a real shocker once you tie the knot.

Our heavenly Father wants us to be dependent upon him,

first and foremost, and he has designed marriage around this principle. A covenant marriage puts God at the center of the marriage, with strengthening one's faith being the main strategy for marital satisfaction and fulfillment.

Imagine a triangle with God at the apex and you and your wife across from each other at the bottom two angles. You can never work hard enough to meet the expectations of your partner because you are human. If you want to have a strong marriage, strengthen your relationship with God. By the way, the quality of your relationship with God will be transparently revealed by the way in which you consistently treat your wife.

Many otherwise strong relationships get in trouble when a husband or wife depends too much on their spouse and not enough on God. Obviously, then, it is imperative that you marry a young woman who understands, appreciates, and is committed to a covenant marriage with you and the Lord. After all, what would you gain if you had everything else working in your favor, but failed to secure a covenant marriage?

Next, I want you to know that soul mates are created, not discovered. There is a lot of social chatter promoting the idea that this celebrity or that reality star has found his or her soul mate. But I side with my good friend clinical psychologist Dr. Mark Crawford, who says, "Soul mates are created, not discovered. The idea of finding your soul mate is a myth. A soul mate is created by sharing the best and worst experiences of life together over a period of many, many years." This is not bad news, and it is the truth.

While God may bring you together, that doesn't automatically make you soul mates, particularly with the idyllic image of soul mates that most people evoke. And even if your wife is your soul mate, what exactly do you believe that means anyway?

I also want you to know that your future marriage, like

the rest of life, will never be all good or all bad. Your future wife will marry a person flawed and gifted in numerous, often unpredictable ways, and so will you. Consequently, nowhere is the apostle Paul's advice from Philippians 4:8 more valuable, more practical, and more enduring than in the arena of marriage. Focus on her strengths more than her weaknesses—what you're glad to have, not what you think is missing.

Inevitably, permanent relationships are filled with peaks and valleys, and maybe a few minefields. But even in the valleys, not everything will be rotten. There will still be some things worth appreciating. And even on the mountain peaks, stresses and struggles will certainly linger. Your marriage can be very, very good, and I pray that it will, but it will not be perfect. Don't expect this.

The long-term success of your marriage will boil down to the concept of love and respect as laid out in Ephesians:

> Husbands, go all out in your love for your wives, exactly as Christ did for the church—a love marked by giving, not getting. Christ's love makes the church whole. His words evoke her beauty. Everything he does and says is designed to bring the best out of her, dressing her in dazzling white silk, radiant with holiness. And that is how husbands ought to love their wives. They're really doing themselves a favor—since they're already "one" in marriage. (Eph. 5:25–28 MSG)

Son, I also want you to know that sex is for marriage. In this day and age, it is hard to imagine that sex was designed by God as a gift for husband and wife to share together. It is my responsibility to share this truth with you because the rest of the world will send a very different message.

There are many practical reasons for saving sex for your

wife, but the most important is that you will get to enjoy what God designed to be the greatest intimate experience between a man and a woman. Purity allows this intimacy to take place. Impurity blocks this capability for intimacy, thereby reducing the joy intended for sex in marriage.

If you choose to have sexual relations outside of marriage, you will likely never comprehend what you missed. You can decide to short-circuit God's plan, but you will settle for less; and as a result of your decision, you will force your spouse to settle as well. Although you probably have not met her yet, remain pure for your wife and pray, as I will continue to do, that she does the same for you.

Your resolve to wait for marriage will be tested, challenged, and ridiculed. The standards for appropriate male-female interaction today are lower than they have ever been. Moral compromise is not the exception but the norm. It is likely that the peer group that you choose will have the greatest influence on whether or not you wait for marriage or follow the crowd. Think about your future wife and make a decision about purity now.

Next, I encourage you to develop clarity early about the qualities you are looking for in a wife. Even if the wedding day is years away, bringing some intentionality into this life experience is helpful. Once you fall in love, a great deal of your capacity to make rational decisions will temporarily evaporate. Take a few minutes and make a list outlining the qualities and attributes you'd like to see reflected in your future wife. Look at this list often and constantly ask yourself if you are becoming the type of man who could attract such a woman as you have described.

Finally, since you were very young, I have been praying for the girl whom you will someday marry. I have prayed for her faith, her integrity, and her safety. I encourage you to begin praying today for the woman God wants you to call your wife at some point down the road. Pray for her now, even though you don't know who or where she is or when you will meet. Ask God to bring you together at the most perfect time. There is no benefit whatsoever in rushing the decision to get married.

God calls us to the extraordinary and invites us to partner with him. This is what God desires to show the world through covenant marriage, son. My prayer is that this is what you've seen in our home and will continue to see in years ahead. It's my prayer that God's desires for you will inspire the desires of your heart for your family and for your future.

Love,

Dad

34

PRACTICE THE 4:8 PRINCIPLE

Dear Brooks,

Not too long ago, one of your brothers procrastinated on his summer reading report for so long that Mom made him work on it while we were at the beach. With eight weeks of summer already gone and no book report in sight, it was finally time for Ty to sit down and crank out the essay. Despite the presence of family, friends, and the sparkling waters of the Gulf of Mexico in the background, we forced him to sit down at the dining-room table, in full view of the beach, telling him that he couldn't do anything else until he was finished. He was not a happy eleven-year-old boy.

I tried to cheer him up, but nothing seemed to work. He said it was the worst vacation ever. After lovingly reminding him that he was responsible for the predicament, I sat down next to him, searching for some way to encourage him without letting him off the hook. I asked him if there was anything else other than the summer reading report that was making him so upset. He said no. Then I asked him if there was anything he was happy about. He again and more emphatically answered no. Of course, I knew in his current state, he was "forgetting" a lot of good things.

Pushing him a little more, I reminded him that if he finished the report today he would have almost a whole week to play and have fun with no more schoolwork. I reminded him that for dinner we'd be eating at Demetrios, his (and now your) favorite pizza restaurant at the beach, and that we'd stop for ice cream on the way back. I reminded him that his grandparents were arriving the next day and that the next week, when we returned to Atlanta, he would still have four days before school started. Finally, his mind-set and facial expression seemed to lighten up a bit.

> God is working thru u 2day

A moment later, when Ty seemed receptive, I asked him if it seemed smart to let just one negative thing determine his entire attitude and the way he felt. He quickly answered no, then asked me to stop bothering him as he put his head down and started writing.

Brooks, if you are not careful, it is easy to get into the mental habit of obsessing about the few things that aren't going well instead of appreciating the *many* things you're grateful for and happy about.

When I was a teenager, your great-grandmother shared with me a certain Bible verse that gripped my attention. As time passed, it amazed me that something so simple could be so powerful. I eventually concluded that this single passage from the New Testament contained within it an essential secret, a principle I had to understand before I could live my best life.

I was hooked.

This secret was not a theoretical proposition, like much of what I had learned in school, but a remarkably practical truth with instant, real-world value. It was an insight that changed my life. As you already know, the verse I am referring to is Philippians 4:8, where the apostle Paul challenges us to seek out and dwell on the good stuff in our lives:

Finally, brethren, whatsoever things are true, whatsoever things are honest, whatsoever things are just, whatsoever things are pure, whatsoever things are lovely, whatsoever things are of good report; if there be any virtue, and if there be any praise, think on these things. (KJV)

In *The Message*, it reads,

Summing it all up, friends, I'd say you'll do best by filling your minds and meditating on things true, noble, reputable, authentic, compelling, gracious—the best, not the worst; the beautiful, not the ugly; things to praise, not things to curse.

Consider this verse carefully for a moment. The very fact that Paul is telling us what we should focus on reveals a critical point: we always have a choice.

If we didn't, this verse would be unnecessary. If we were naturally positive all the time, Paul wouldn't emphasize this point so dramatically. If we could not control our negativity, this teaching would be in vain, unrealistic, and beyond our capability. Paul is reminding us that *we have a choice*. With God's help, we can control our thoughts. Further, his words teach us that the choice is between good and bad, between excellence and mediocrity.

As you've grown up, you have learned that life has its good times and its bad times. There are the unavoidable ups and downs. The greatest of lives are filled with both victory and defeat, with both struggles and successes. School is a mixture of good and bad. So too are friendships and football. Our neighborhood, as well as our nation, is a mixture of good and bad.

Likewise, growing up is a mixture of good and bad. Your future career will be a mixture of good and bad. Down the road, you will discover that marriage is also a mixture of good and bad. In fact, your entire life here on earth is a mixture of both positive and negative things.

While I am sure this makes sense to you, I want to emphasize that the good times and the bad times are going to be happening all the time. Maybe you just aced your chemistry test, but then you fumbled the ball and missed an easy touchdown only a few hours later. Maybe the girl you wanted to ask out just said yes, right before you accidentally dropped your phone in the pool. Maybe a good friend disappointed you, but a few minutes later you found out you got accepted to your first choice for college. There will always be some junk, and there will always be some greatness.

Inevitably, your future will include both peaks and valleys. But even in the valleys, there will always be something working really well in your life; and even on the mountain peaks, everything will not be perfect. As your life unfolds, I assure you there will always be something to complain about, but far more important, you will always have some blessings to count. What you focus on will be your choice and your choice alone.

At any given moment, you can choose to pay attention to what you have or what you don't have, what's working or what's broken, what you achieved or what you messed up, what's possible or what's impossible, and what excites you or what frightens you. No area of your life will remain untouched by the thoughts you choose to think.

Following Paul's advice will help you become mentally disciplined. And mental discipline will allow you to experience emotional discipline. In other words, your feelings are a side effect of your thought life. Happy feelings grow from happy thoughts. Sad feelings are the consequence of sad thoughts.

Confidence arises from confident thinking. You will always feel what you focus upon.

The more frequently you think about something, the tighter the grip it exerts on you, the decisions you make, and the actions you take. And over the long haul, your life will tend to reproduce in reality the thoughts that you hold most consistently. Like most of the world, you have hundreds of problems and millions of blessings! Whether you choose to count your blessings or choose to complain about what is wrong with your life, know that *you do have a choice.*

Brooks, every day may not be good, but if you look for it, you will be able to find something good in every day. Focus on the good stuff.

Practice the 4:8 principle!

Love,

Dad

35

FOLLOW YOUR PASSION

Dear Zach,

She lost her left arm and 60 percent of her blood. Doctors called her survival a miracle. But thirteen-year-old Bethany Hamilton refused to surrender her passion for surfing after being attacked by a fourteen-foot tiger shark off of Kauai's North Shore. Instead, she returned to the water and reclaimed her passion. Bolstered by her faith, she transformed her personal adversity into public inspiration for millions.

There are two ways to go through life—either with passion or without. The challenge is that life tends to steer us down the popular path and not the particular path God made for us. With passion, we move forward toward God's purpose for our life. Without passion, we conform to the crowd, stick to the status quo, and bury our uniqueness. Consequently, we miss out on a blessing so extraordinary that it's hard to even describe unless we have personally experienced it.

No doubt about it, passion is life as it was meant to be. It infuses your time here on earth with the joy that can only come from living the specific life God gave *you*. Positive passion is an emotional blessing that fills you with the enthusiasm to persist through, around, or over the difficulties and hardships of life.

Like love or hate, we can possess healthy as well as unhealthy passions. Your passions tell a lot about who you are and even more about who you will become. Men become devoted to their passions; therefore, be careful and wise. Just as healthy passions can accelerate your progress, unhealthy passions can accelerate your demise. Our healthy passions are the wings that carry us to the life we imagine. These intense, overriding feelings and convictions energize us with the emotional fuel to pursue and accomplish amazing things. When you're positively passionate, you are wide-awake, fully engaged, and completely alive. This full-throttle approach to life is the only way to go.

Positive passion is the spiritual and emotional force that drives us toward becoming the person God envisioned when he created us. To a very large degree, life and passion are really one and the same. If you're not passionate about something, you're not really living at all. You may have a pulse, a job, and even some hobbies, but you're only going through the motions if you're not following your passion.

Your passion is the compelling and irresistible goal or cause or vision that you hunger to bring into reality. Identifying and following this passion makes the good times great and the bad times not quite so bad. Satisfying this passion is a labor of love that energizes

> Never give up . . . never

you spiritually, emotionally, mentally, and physically. Passion inspires you to get up early and stay up late, working toward something significant. Nothing quite matches the sense of aliveness that comes from living and giving with passion. It is infectious, contagious, and strangely attractive.

Growing up, I had a passion for baseball. I ate, slept, and dreamt about it. If I wasn't playing or practicing baseball, I wanted to watch someone else play. If I couldn't do that, I wanted to talk about baseball or read about my baseball heroes. Thinking, talking, watching, and especially playing baseball kept me fully engaged, excited, and motivated to reach my potential. That's what a passion is like.

Some people are passionate about their faith. Some people are passionate about selling. Some people are passionate about their kids. Some people are passionate about making furniture or rock climbing. Others are passionate about teaching or curing illnesses. Some people are passionate about preserving freedom or solving crimes. Some people are passionate about technology while others are passionate about winning championships. Other people are passionate about making their communities better places to live.

My hope for you is that you too will develop a hunger to make a difference in the world, not just a hunger to make a living in the workforce. If so, this appetite will naturally flow from your passion. One of the greatest, if not the single greatest, responsibility you have in life, Zach, is to discover what God put you here on earth to accomplish. This means following your dreams and using your strengths to make the difference that only you are uniquely qualified to make.

Of course, voices along the way will urge you to turn back and take a safer path—even voices of doubt and discouragement from within yourself. Don't let negativity from yourself or others deter you. Instead, listen to the voice of truth. Press on toward the goal. Live and give with passion. When you choose to run with the dream God planted in your heart, you must be willing to surrender safety, security, and comfort in exchange for the higher reward of living the life God uniquely created for you so you could leave your unmistakable mark on the world. Remember, conformity is the greatest threat to a life of passion.

I've seen plenty of people with passion but no purpose, but rarely have I observed an individual who has purpose but no passion. Everyone knows human beings need food, water, and oxygen. But people are also created with a driving need for passion rooted in a purpose for being alive. Without this passion, people feel insignificant and unfocused, gradually becoming more interested in escaping life than really living it.

This isn't as obvious when you're still in school and often being told what to do and where to be. But it becomes a much bigger deal once you have the total freedom to follow your own path in life. The passionate life pays extra rewards and naturally comes with a higher price tag.

Zach, God created you to place a unique stamp on his creation. God wants to do big things through your life. Don't conform to an average life. God's will for you is something far bigger than anything you could imagine for yourself. You've been custom designed by God to serve a unique function in his world, and your passion lights the way.

I have observed that the intensity of a man's passion is in direct proportion to the size of his dream. Little goals require and therefore produce little passion. God-sized goals demand and therefore generate huge passion for their attainment.

I encourage you to follow your passion and pursue the dream God planted in your heart. It is the greatest clue to how God wants you to invest your life. While there may be delays, detours, and disappointments along the way, never let anyone smear that picture or deflate that passion.

So what's your dream, Zach? What's your passion? What do you want your life to be about? What do you want your life to stand for?

Follow your passion, son!

Love,
Dad

36

MAKE NO EXCUSE

Dear Mason,

The old Paralympics slogan says it all: "What's Your Excuse?" Questions are often the best teachers because they prompt us to think. When we're told something, we're likely to smile politely and let our thoughts drift to another subject. But questions captivate us because we're conditioned to answer them.

So ask yourself, "What is my excuse?" Think about the parts of your life that aren't quite the way you'd like them to be. Think about your faith, your family, your friends, your school work, and your sports. Think about the excuses you've given others and those you've silently told yourself. Unfortunately for all of us, while we're making excuses, other people are making progress.

I remember the first time I heard the classic excuse "My dog ate my homework" from a third-grade classmate who didn't even have a dog. The entire class, including the teacher, broke out in laughter. I don't remember whether the excuse did what my classmate hoped it would do, but I do remember the laughter and the embarrassment on his face. Looking back, I realize how appropriate the laughter was. Excuses deserve laughter, not dignity. Excuses and responsibility can't coexist. It's easy to say, "I'm not responsible," and hard to say, "I am responsible." If there are things in your life that aren't the way you want them to be, you and only you are responsible for changing them. It's up to you to create solutions to life's challenges, whether big or small.

Each time you make an excuse, you diminish your respect, your credibility, and your integrity. Each time you make an excuse, you reinforce your inclination to make more excuses in the future, and excuse making can quickly become a habit.

Commit to making your home, car, classroom and athletic field excuse-free zones. When you're tempted to make an excuse, substitute the words *I am responsible*. Look to yourself for the cause of your problems or missteps. If you're not happy with your results, accept responsibility for them. Whether it is academics, sports, friendships, or faith, *it's your life*. Sometimes bad things can happen despite your good intentions or thorough preparations. Accidents are a part of life. Evil is real. And other people can use their free will to inflict damage in your life. Sometimes you may have no control to change or immediately fix these kinds of situations. You will find over your lifetime, however, that these situations are the minority of your circumstances. In most cases, either you passively allowed the unacceptable circumstance to come about, or you actively created it. This reality can be difficult to come to terms with, but accepting responsibility isn't an invitation to beat up on yourself. Instead, it's an opportunity to see the truth about how and why you got to be where you are. Acknowledging the truth is the only path to a future that's better than the past.

When a circumstance doesn't work out the way you'd hoped, claim responsibility and ask yourself, "What could I have done to avoid this problem?" For instance, imagine opening your refrigerator and taking out the orange juice. Following the instructions on the label, you shake the carton vigorously—only to have the cap fly off and orange juice spew all over you, the counters, the floor, and even the ceiling. At this point, you have two options:

1. You can blame the knucklehead who didn't screw on the cap properly after he used the juice and demand that he help you clean up.
2. You can remind yourself that this mess could have been avoided altogether if you had only checked the cap before you started shaking the carton. Of course, it would have been considerate if the person who'd put away the juice had secured the cap, but the power to prevent this situation was also in your hands.

Taking responsibility for your life is like being a defensive driver. If your car is totaled in an accident, you won't get much comfort from the fact that you had the green light. That's just an excuse. Blaming the other driver won't help either; it will only pull your attention away from what you need to learn. Your first question should be, "What could I have done to prevent this?" When you analyze unpleasant situations from the perspective of what *you* can do to keep them from happening again, you remain in control and empowered.

The only thing more damaging to your success than making excuses is making the same excuse twice. Remember, there is never enough room for both "buts" and brilliance. You must make the choice. At the end of the day, whether walking off the baseball field or walking across the stage at graduation, do you want to know all you offered was "Yeah, but," or do you want to see that you gave your best to reach your goal?

Make your entire life an excuse-free zone, and you'll reach your goals and have a blast in the process.

Love you,

Dad

37

SOW, THEN REAP

Dear Trey,

The day you were born, I held you in my arms and looked into your face and thanked God for giving you to your mom and me. But I also wondered what you'd be like as you grew up. Would you like baseball or golf? Would you be a talker or the quiet one? Would you want to fly airplanes, work on computers, tinker with engines, or be a wilderness guide some day? I would have loved to have snuck a peek into the future to see the good things that would come one day for you.

There's a desire built inside each of us to look into the future. We all hope that something good is coming our way and to those we love. Well, I'm going to let you in on a little secret, Trey. God's given all of us the power to foretell the future when we apply one simple principle: today's choices predict tomorrow's successes and failures.

This statement is true because we live in an orderly universe governed by laws that work the same way for all of us, no matter who we are, time and time again.

One of my favorite authors, James Allen, put it like this: "Good thoughts and actions can never produce bad results; bad thoughts and actions can never produce good results."[1] The principle of sowing and reaping is as simple as one plus one equals two: first we sow, and then we reap. The same equation applies to all of us. Like gravity, the principle works all day, every day, in every corner of the universe, regardless of whether we're aware of it or not.

It's impossible to sow irresponsibility and harvest integrity. It's impossible to sow dishonor and harvest respect. It's impossible to sow mediocrity and harvest excellence. But millions of people refuse to believe this simple truth. Far too many people in our nation squander their lives. They hope to reap productivity, excellence, and prosperity when they have not sown effort, and they grow bitter when they do not receive the fruit they did not plant. They do not understand that the fruit we harvest comes from the seeds we sow.

An ancient parable in Matthew 13:1–8 reminds us that we'd be wise to plant a bit more than we hope to harvest. This is because some of the seed won't bear any fruit at all. This is not an injustice, and it doesn't make us victims. It's just another mysterious dynamic of life.

Think about ur future

According to the story, some percentage of the seeds we sow will be taken by the birds, some will land on the rocky ground and shrivel in the heat, and some will be strangled by the weeds. Others will take root in the fertile soil and yield a lopsided crop—a hundred, sixty, or even thirty times what was sown. The message is clear: plant more seeds of wisdom, love, service, value, productivity, and grace than you will ever possibly need. Let your focus be on the planting and leave the harvest to God.

Once we're aware of this dynamic, we can fine-tune our life strategies to be in harmony with it. In athletics, you are free to plant more practice seeds than your teammates or competitors. In school, you can study as much as the teacher recommends, or you can choose to plant extra learning seeds. It is up to you. If you enter the business world and want to be highly paid, you must first become highly valuable in the eyes of the person who signs your check. You must show that you bring qualities that contribute to the organization and can push it toward its desired goals. In order to do that, you will need to be willing to sow more than you hope to harvest.

Trey, many Americans have been deceived into thinking they're not accountable for their choices. They don't understand that behaviors and consequences are related. They've been told that all choices are equal and shouldn't give anyone an "unfair" advantage. But all choices are not created equal. Those who choose to study more, practice more, create more, and serve more achieve more for obvious reasons.

Our nation has invested millions of dollars in research for medical cures for illnesses, as well as social problems that are linked to our physical, emotional, and economic health. But we're reluctant to address the root causes of many of those problems: individual choices. And why? Because talking about root causes of problems that are connected to moral choices has been labeled as judgmental, insensitive, politically incorrect, and narrow-minded. But we have forgotten that both action and inaction have consequences, and consequences are most often our best teachers.

Your success in life will never be based on the needs you perceive, but rather on the seeds you plant. You will be faced with the choice of becoming either a first-rate planter who plans and plants in the spring, or a clever beggar who relies on the efforts of others in the fall. Your success will be the product of strategic thinking, combined with positive action. Success comes from a goal, a plan, and massive action toward your goal. Success is not an accident. Success does not come randomly; it is the reward of targeted effort. Oswald Chambers sums up the ultimate measure of success: "God's call is for you to be his loyal friend, to accomplish his purposes and goals for your life."[2] Sow this truth into the fabric of your life, Trey, and you will reap a harvest of true success. Tomorrow changes today. Today holds the key to your future. The work of success begins today.

Love,

Dad

38

BELIEVE IN FREE ENTERPRISE

Zach,

Being born in America is a blessing with an incalculable price tag. You are growing up in a country where anyone can make it and anyone can lose it. Because of free enterprise, individuals can envision a better future, set a goal, serve others, take some risks, and flourish. The free market allows this opportunity, but it does not mandate results. You are free to both succeed and fail. Disappointingly, this is a point of contention for many.

As I am writing this note, there are a growing number of Americans who are drifting away from the mind-set of opportunity and creeping toward the mind-set of entitlement. There is a legitimate concern that economic freedom as we have known it and the blessings it generously scatters across our land are at risk of extinction.

Please understand that America has provided more opportunity for more people to realize their dreams than any other country in history. The United States was designed for the common man with a dream, as opposed to the already rich and powerful. The systems of law and commerce were set up to reward self-reliance, entrepreneurship, and individual responsibility.

America has been and is still today the platform that allows and encourages the average to become exceptional. There is no other place on the planet that is designed to help industrious people get more of what they want in life. Consequently, the opportunity for economic success here is unmatched. But it is just that—an opportunity, not an entitlement.

The concept of a free market is quite simple. It does not involve compulsion or coercion. You and all individuals have the right to enter the market and sell your goods or services for whatever amount other people are willing to pay. No one is forced to buy, and no one is forced to sell. Getting the things you want in life will require that you create something that others want and then sell it to them at a price that makes them want to buy it. You may end up selling your time to an employer or your product to a customer, but it is essentially the same process.

This model is based on cooperation and voluntary exchange. If you want more money, then you need to serve more people and add more value to them in order to earn those rewards. Remember it like this: the more enterprising you are, the more freedom you can experience. The preceding sentence is worth rereading.

People trade their money for a product or service because they believe they will be better off with the product or service than with the money they used to buy it. And the seller believes he'll be better off with the profit than with the product or service he sold. Both parties expect to be in a better position after the trade.

These elementary free-market concepts have always been America's primary economic principles. We take our talents, skills, and other assets to the market and sell them for as much as someone else is willing to pay for them. When we serve others well, they reward us well. When we add value to fellow citizens, they help us become more prosperous.

The free market has turned America into an incomparably

affluent country—no other large country even comes close to our per-capita wealth. Still, critics condemn the disparity between the poor and the prosperous. And there's no doubt that some Americans are struggling and that society needs a safety net for them. But critics of capitalism tend not to mention that even the poor have it far better in America than virtually anywhere else.

The free market is inextricably linked to our quality of life. Ever wondered why a wildly disproportionate amount of the technological progress of the last hundred years has happened in the United States? It's because free enterprise encourages risk taking, reward achieving, creative breakthroughs, and scientific exploration. Is this dumb luck? Have Americans won a planetary lottery? Of course not! We are blessed, indeed, but our success is no accident: progress and excellence thrive in a free market.

Go the extra mile 2day

The way capitalism works is a lot like being a server in a restaurant. Servers have an opportunity to earn a good tip. This is not an entitlement, just a possibility. Likewise, an entrepreneur, maybe the restaurateur in this case, has an opportunity to get wealthy. Again, there is no guarantee, just a possibility. Anything the server can do to go the extra mile will increase the likelihood of a nice tip for himself, and more business for the restaurateur.

For the server to successfully draw a generous tip, he needs to provide the one-two punch of personality and performance while exceeding the expectations of the guest. This means the server needs to know the menu, understand the restaurant's operating system, be attentive but not intrusive, and develop a positive rapport with the potential tippers. If he does this, he'll receive a generous gratuity 95 percent of the time.

For the restaurant owner to be successful, she must risk her capital, create a unique dining experience, offer good food at a price potential customers are willing to pay, and exceed expectations during each subsequent visit. Should she accomplish these objectives, she has a great shot of reaching her financial goals, but still no guarantee. Anything the restaurateur can do to travel that lonely second mile will improve her chances of becoming wealthy.

Zach, while capitalism is no doubt imperfect, it has proven itself to be far better at creating more abundance for more people than any other economic system. I encourage you to become a champion for the free market, and in the process you will also be preserving the great American idea for future generations.

Love,
Dad

39

STAY HUMBLE

Trey,

Each time I tell you how proud I am of you, the thing I admire most is the quality of humility you possess and project to others. Some people misunderstand what humility is all about. It's not thinking less or negatively about yourself. It's about seeing yourself the way God sees you. When you share God's opinion about you, you're free to be confident in your strengths because you're relying on the true source of your power, and you're free to acknowledge your weaknesses without demeaning and criticizing yourself.

You will never be sinless or live a sinless life. But God, in his grace, sees you as blameless. Every good thing you will ever become flows from the good gifts he's seeded into your life. The humble man never loses awareness of his dependence upon God. Gratitude, humility, and an attitude of repentance are the three-strand cord that binds his heart. When you experience God's goodness in your life, there is no need to feel guilty, but there is a responsibility to express gratitude. Continuous thanksgiving goes a long way toward keeping your heart humble.

It's okay if you don't always feel like being humble; just do it anyway. Let your results and other people speak for you. God knows what you've accomplished, warts and all. Remember, people are drawn to those who project confidence without trying to inflate themselves, hog the glory, or be right all the time. You'll notice that the less approval or glory you try to create for yourself, the more of it comes to you naturally.

It's not good enough to read your Bible, go to church, do good things for your friends and community, and try not to sin. That's pretty much what the Pharisees in the Bible did. God asks you to develop character qualities that reflect his character. Micah 6:8 gives you your job description for life, Ty: do justice, love mercy, and walk humbly with God.

First, do justice: treat people with honor. Fight oppression. Defend the defenseless. Second, love mercy: feed the hungry. Visit prisoners. Show compassion. Third, in all things, walk humbly with God. When you invest intimate time with him, humility will become a natural byproduct of your life. I have lots of very successful friends from all walks of life, but those I respect the most and seek for counsel are those who have succeeded with humility.

The legendary basketball coach John Wooden put it well when he said, "Talent is God given. Be humble. Fame is man-given. Be grateful. Conceit is self-given. Be careful."[1]

Love,
Dad

40

BE AWARE OF 80/20 THINKING

Ty,

More than one hundred years ago the Italian economist Vilfredo Pareto discovered what is now commonly referred to as the 80/20 principle. The purpose of this note is to get you curious about this simple principle that can transform how you think, plan, work, exercise, relax, and otherwise participate in and add value to the world.

A lot of people have heard of the 80/20 principle, but very few individuals, outside of the business world, put it to use in their lives. Even in the marketplace, this principle is rarely used. I am sharing this insight with you because I believe it can give you an advantage, if not at this moment, then very soon—and especially after you exit the world of academia.

View the 80/20 principle as an amazing thought stimulator that can not only help you make faster progress toward your goals but also help you make more sense out the world in which you live. Your early awareness of this maxim will sharpen your thinking and activate your imagination. So what is it? you ask. Well, the 80/20 principle tells us that most of what we do has limited value and some of what we do has tremendous value. I suspect this sounds a little funny to you.

Nonetheless, most of our activity or efforts have little impact on the end result or goal we are striving toward. Interestingly, a few efforts have enormous impact. The key, then, is to know where to focus. Once we identify what works really well, we should multiply it. When we identify activities, tasks, or methods that are not very productive, we should eliminate or neutralize them as best we can. You can apply this thinking to your schoolwork, sports training, and how you organize yourself to accomplish the things that are important to you.

Assuming no outside or artificial interference, results in life will be predictably imbalanced. There is a naturally lopsided relationship between cause and consequence. We can burn our time wishing this were not so, or we can use our ingenuity to align our lives to be in harmony with it. I encourage you to choose the latter.

It sounds sort of crazy, but trust me on this one: the vast majority of what you or I do makes very little difference, especially in the long run. On the other hand, a small number of our actions have a huge impact. In most businesses, for example, 80 percent of the revenue is generated by only 20 percent of the sales force, meaning the team's success relies on a small, super-productive minority.

But how do they accomplish this? With rare exception, it is impossible for anyone to be ten or twenty times smarter than someone else. We know these star salespeople don't have ten or twenty times more time available. Therefore, they must approach their goals differently. They must have a better way to achieve such results.

You have already noticed this lopsided dynamic when playing football and other sports. While it may take the whole team to win a game, there are always two or three players (about 20 percent) who are disproportionately better than everyone else.

Without this minority of highly valuable players, winning would be nearly impossible. From this minority of exceptional athletes there will usually be one who stands out even more, and that person is selected as the *most valuable* player.

Wondering how you can apply 80/20 thinking sooner rather than later? Here's a hint: you can never do everything; therefore, you must figure out what are the most valuable priorities and execute them consistently. Ask yourself what will give you a much better result with much less effort. This may sound like lazy thinking at first, but instead, it is the beginning of transformational thinking.

This principle and the mind-set it produces help explain why some people are exponentially more successful than others. Unfortunately, only a tiny fraction of the working population applies this law of productivity in their work, and even fewer do so in their family lives, despite the dramatic breakthroughs that are possible.

As a student, what are the two or three things that contribute the most to earning good grades? Focus on these things. As an athlete, what are one or two fundamentals that will make you a disproportionately better player if you mastered them? Focus on these things. This principle will make

> What r ur strengths?

even more sense to you when you get out of school because the world of academics largely ignores this principle, and in many cases it practices the opposite, as you have already experienced firsthand.

With good intentions, most schools still demand that students become generalists, becoming proficient with a wide range of subject matter, regardless of aptitude or interest. Furthermore, typical school days allocate time evenly across most subjects, meaning the most valuable subjects receive the same allotment of time as the least valuable. This is, by and large, the same model used for the last one hundred plus years. While there is nothing inherently wrong with teaching younger kids an assortment of subjects or dividing the day into equal parts, it doesn't prepare you for the work world that you will eventually be entering.

When you scatter your attention across too many different subjects, your ability to demonstrate excellence in any one discipline is diminished. Consequently, the weaker areas are highlighted and often require special efforts and the areas of excellence can get ignored. This may be a satisfactory approach for the school years, but it won't produce optimal results later in life, when you will be allowed, but not compelled, to focus on your strengths.

I challenge you to start observing this phenomenon as you wrap up school. Like your mom, you could even start experimenting with your own 80/20 theories. She accuses me of wearing 20 percent of my shirts 80 percent of the time. Hmmm . . .

Love,
Dad

41

BUILD CHARACTER FROM WITHIN

Zach,

A story I heard as a boy speaks to our nation's condition today. It went like this: Little Scotty wanted to play with his dad, but his dad wanted to read his massive Sunday paper. Well, Scotty kept tapping on the news- paper to get his father's attention until his father finally had an idea. He tore a page out of the paper that showed a map of the world, ripping it into puzzle pieces as he said, "As soon as you put this picture together, I'll play with you."

Two minutes later his son showed up with the picture pieced back together again. His dad was surprised and responded, "Scotty, how did you put this picture of the whole world together so fast?"

Scotty replied, "Daddy, it was easy. There was a picture of a man on the other side. If you put the man together right, the world goes together just fine."

We can learn from Scotty's example. We hear a lot about society's problems in America today, but we seldom hear about real solutions. Why do large segments of America continue to look to the federal government to fix society when the government has such a terrible track record of fixing anything? The part people seem to miss is the fact that "society's" problems are individual people's problems. Society is nothing more than a group of people, and people problems always boil down to character problems that must be solved on the individual level. Instead of trying to rebuild health care or rebuild the economy, our first priority should be to address the need for building individual character.

A government that has chosen to reject its moral roots cannot instill morality within its citizens. It cannot even provide a moral example. The role of instilling individual character belongs to the family and the church, and a wise government would enthusiastically support efforts to encourage its citizens to be more honest, trustworthy, diligent, committed to family, self-sacrificing, and honorable.

But the ball rests with you, son. Why me? you ask. Because it's your job to become a man of character and to build character within your family someday. It's your job to become a person of initiative and influence your community. Don't wait for government to change your world. Become the man you hope to see leading your nation.

The solution lies at the heart of our nation; we take the initiative to become the solution. This is the formula for real change because real change comes from within.

The question for all of us and for you, son, is, what are you doing today that will bring positive change in your life and in your nation tomorrow?

Dad

42

LIVE WITH COMPASSION

Zach,

Compassion is a feeling of sympathy for others. Like personal responsibility, work ethic, and integrity, compassion is a trait possessed by men of high character. This doesn't mean you are naturally compassionate; in fact, it is more likely that you will have to consciously practice to build up your compassion throughout your life.

Compassion is recognizing another person's pain at the moment, rather than judging what they did, didn't do, or could have done to avoid their circumstances. We are compassionate when we zero in on other people's hurts and think about them, speak to them, or act toward them the way we would want to be treated if the circumstances were reversed.

It is easy to get swept up in our own circumstances and become so self-absorbed that we miss or don't pay attention to the people around us. Make compassion a priority. Look for opportunities to offer compassion, both to strangers and especially to those closest to you. Sometimes compassion is simply withholding criticism or judgment and instead offering a silent prayer for the person in need. Sometimes compassion may demand your time or money or effort. Sometimes it will require only a smile, a handshake, or a second chance.

Compassion is offering help and comfort because we

empathize with the other person, partially because we are grateful we are not in their position. The more gratitude we show for our blessings, the more compassionate we'll tend to be toward others who find themselves in tough conditions. The more grateful we feel for our own blessings and abundance, the more compassion we express toward others who are struggling in difficult circumstances.

We all have stories, son. And it's easy to go through life making assumptions about people and their circumstances. It's much harder to crawl out of your skin and your limited perspective and live with compassion. It takes a decision of both your will and emotions to live with compassion. Extending compassion requires you to learn to see others outside your own limited framework of experience.

While it is important to show compassion to those in need halfway around the world, I challenge you to focus plenty of compassion on those closest to us. Show compassion for your friends. Show compassion for your

Make smart choices

teachers. Once you're married, show compassion for your wife. And please show compassion for your mom and me. Don't save all your compassion just for the dramatic causes of our time; pour out your compassion for your family, for your friends, and for those who love you unconditionally and with whom you are investing your life.

Choose compassion because it is a biblically sound virtue that consequently produces biblically sanctioned fruit. There is really nothing to lose when taking this approach, but there is much to gain.

Living with compassion is an adventure, son. It will take you to exciting places you never dreamed possible because it is a dynamic force that breaks down walls of separation, isolation, deception, and apathy between individuals, families, genera-tions, and cultures.

In your lifetime, I pray that you are going to be blessed with a continuous flow of compassion from others. Many will express compassion when you are dealing with heartbreaking circumstances out of your own control, such as the sudden loss of a loved one. Others will show you compassion despite the fact that it was your own poor choices that landed you in an ugly predicament.

You will need these kinds of people in your life. Ask God for an abundance of compassionate friends and allies to surround you on your journey through life. Then make it a priority to become that type of person yourself.

Compassion holds the key to living with joy and creating joy in the lives of others. Pursue it, practice it, and make it the bedrock reflex of your life.

Love you,
Dad

43

ACTIVATE THE REALITY PRINCIPLE

Trey,

You must learn to deal with the world the way it really is, not the way you wish it was. I call this the reality principle. But in order to be able to deal with the world, you'll need to understand how it works. Study history. Uncover the facts. Seek the truth. Remain objective. As John Adams liked to say, "Facts are stubborn things." Until you understand how the world works and where you are compared to where you'd rather be, you won't be free to move forward with wisdom and improve your situation. This holds true for your business career, your marriage, your health, and every other aspect of your life. You must learn to discriminate between unalterable facts and solvable problems.

Facing reality means you look at things honestly. You "tell it like it is," not like you wish things were. You demonstrate intellectual honesty—no games, no blaming, no name-calling, or hiding behind flimsy arguments. You acknowledge the truth, even if it's ugly and means owning up to your share of responsibility.

People who understand the reality principle don't have

`Carve ur own path`

patience for political correctness. They don't label certain topics off-limits or censor people from stating the truth. They know that freedom to follow the truth changes everything; and without freedom to follow the truth, you can never know reality in the first place.

People who understand the reality principle take the time to look at the big picture. Often you'll need to step back from your circumstances so you can see the whole picture. If you've made mistakes, ask for forgiveness, accept the consequences, and move on.

The more brutally honest you are with yourself, the more effective you can be in correcting your course on the path to your goals. Ask yourself questions. Where are you in life compared to where you want to be? What obstacles today are blocking your goals for tomorrow? What steps can you take to correct your course?

Don't allow yourself to be deceived, son. Look at the world and inventory your gifts, your challenges, and your circumstances. Take a look at reality and ask God for wisdom as you move ahead. Then step forward as he gives you direction.

Dad

44

TAP INTO "THE FIFTEEN"

Ty,

By now, you have already experienced how easy it is to squander time, mainly through school work and sports—and, on the flip side, how easy it is to use it wisely. I wanted to leave you a note briefly describing one of the greatest and simplest practices I have ever learned. I think of it as "The Fifteen."

Here's how it works. Identify something important to you, such as something you want to, or need to, learn or master. Maybe it is advance preparation for an exam or a book you want to read, or a particular move you want to experiment with in lacrosse. Alternatively, you could identify a big project of some kind that is too big to tackle all at once.

As soon as you have selected a focus, the project, or whatever it is you want to master, work on it for fifteen minutes daily until you achieve the result you desire. Embarrassingly, that is all there is to it.

Here is the amazing part, though. (At least it is to me.) In a week, your fifteen minutes will accrue to one hour and forty-five minutes. In a month, it can add up to seven and a half hours. In a quarter, it builds to twenty-two and a half hours. And in a year, your fifteen-minute daily investment accumulates into ninety hours of productive action. And three years from now, those fifteen short minutes will add up to more than eleven extra twenty-four-hour days or thirty extra nine-hour days. How much do you think I could earn selling an extra month of time on eBay?

I know you have some big goals you're moving toward right now. What if you started applying The Fifteen to your goal? Is your goal worth waking up fifteen minutes earlier for? In light of your current circumstances and your future hopes and dreams, what is the best use of this "extra" fifteen minutes? I challenge you to re-budget just fifteen minutes a day, seven days a week to an activity of higher value. By higher value, I mean an activity that is likely to generate something helpful to your life, especially in the long run.

If you give it some thought and you're patient, just fifteen minutes a day will gradually alter your life for the better. If you look diligently, I'm confident you can find this "extra" fifteen minutes somewhere in your day. Consider the beginning or ending of each day. Possibly you could shave fifteen minutes off your lunch routine, especially once you start working full-time. Three months from now, those fifteen extra minutes accumulate to twenty-two and a half bonus hours, or about half of a typical work week.

Practice this quick time habit for the next ten years of your life and you'll tap into one hundred bonus nine-hour days, or more than a quarter of life that otherwise would likely go wasted. Just think about what might happen if you doubled the investment to thirty minutes daily. Fortunately, you already have these extra days, but how will you choose to invest them?

It's worth thinking about because it is the time of your life!

Dad

45

DISCIPLINE YOURSELF
OR THE WORLD WILL

Dear Mason,

In the world of competitive running, few teams draw as much admiration as the father-son pairing known as Team Hoyt. Dick Hoyt described himself as a "porker" before his eleven-year-old, wheelchair-bound son Rick asked him to push him in a charity benefit race twenty-five years ago. The request changed both their lives. Today Dick and Rick have competed in more than a thousand marathons, including thirty Boston Marathons. Dick is now seventy-two and still pushing his fifty-year-old son in a wheelchair, carrying him on a specially built bicycle, and pulling him through the water in a boat by a bungee cord.

So what's the driving force behind Dick Hoyt's self-discipline? I believe it was a father's passion to see his son freed from the limitations of his imperfect body. Love for his son drove Dick Hoyt to dedicate his life to training.

Interestingly, Dick Hoyt was a different, less disciplined man before Rick asked him to help him compete in his first race. But self-discipline is a learned skill, and Dick chose to not only learn it but to triumph over it. He directed his appetites and passions toward competitive racing for the sake of his son.

I am telling you this because, unfortunately, some people believe self-discipline just isn't their thing. They believe some people have it and other people don't. But they're wrong. Self-discipline is an equal-opportunity character trait because it can be learned. It's the ability to funnel our desires and passions in a productive direction for a sustained period of time in order to accomplish what it takes to achieve our goals. Self-discipline is an investment in our future, and it inspires others. Ask the thousands of people in the crowds year after year who come to watch Team Hoyt race—no matter where they may place in competition.

Self-discipline shapes success because it influences choices— small and large—and produces daily momentum that pushes you toward your goals. Self-discipline helps you synchronize your goals with your choices and keeps you moving in the direction of your vision. Right now, your commitment to self-discipline can determine your options for college, your athletic achievements, the privileges you earn, and the foundation of character you build. Later in life, your self-discipline will influence your finances, your marriage, your parenting, your career, your spiritual health, your physical health, and just about everything else. No area of your life will remain untouched by self-discipline.

Self-discipline is the ability to direct your desires and passions in productive ways. Self-discipline is the connective tissue that links ambition with achievement. Mastering self-discipline is like strapping rocket boosters to your vision and goals. It helps take you where you want to go faster and easier, and makes it possible for you to get more out of life along the way. Self-discipline will even help you do the things you dislike better; this is because it will teach you to do hard things more efficiently, and you'll dislike them less because they'll become more manageable.

People often want to take shortcuts to success, but success demands character, and character demands self-discipline. If you learn to value self-discipline and harness its power, you will stand head and shoulders above the rest of the crowd. The young man who understands self-discipline becomes a master of his potential. He knows who he is, who he is not, and who he is focused on becoming, in spite of circumstances. He's the product of his own initiative and doesn't rely upon the resources of others. He knows how to accomplish what needs to be done without a teacher, boss, parent, coach, or supervisor looking over his shoulder to make sure he's done his job and done it with excellence. This is the kind of man you are becoming, Mason.

God gave us biblical examples to help us see the causes and effects of our decisions. Daniel is a biblical role model who exemplified self-discipline. Self-discipline allowed Daniel to rise above the limitations of imprisonment, even when he was physically behind bars. He refused to allow other people's actions or his difficult circumstances to shape his attitude or choices. Instead, he responded to even the most painful and unjust circumstances by channeling his desires, abilities, talents, and gifts in positive ways. Rather than allowing a negative attitude to lure him into self-indulgent choices, Daniel chose intentionality. He chose to

I am very proud of u!

follow his mission over his mood. Self-discipline gave him the power to sustain a positive attitude over the long haul because he refused to be the victim of his circumstances. So where does self-discipline shift from being a conversation to a lifestyle? How can you actually develop it as part of your life? The answer is as simple as making a decision and backing it up with action. Self-discipline is developed by moving forward one step at a time and creating momentum in small, daily acts. The first step is to recognize you're not a slave to your feelings. Guess what, Mason? You can still make positive, goal-directed choices in spite of your emotions.

Most people get tangled up in bad decisions because they don't understand this reality. Undisciplined people are slaves to their feelings, so they experience problems and frustrations that self-disciplined people avoid. Don't get me wrong. Problems and frustrations will inevitably come in your life—in your education, your profession, your relationships, your family life. Everyone faces problems. Those with self-discipline, however, experience far less self-inflicted adversity. Everything you value will require self-discipline to keep it from stagnating and to push it forward in a positive direction, whether that goal is an academic degree, relationship success, advancing your career, achieving financial security, or raising responsible, self-reliant children.

No matter what your goals may be, your commitment to self-discipline will keep you focused on your intentions and off your fears and worries. Self-discipline spurs you to do what you need to do when you need to do it, whether you feel like it or not. Understand that future change is an illusion and a myth. Tomorrow changes only as a result of what you do today.

Sadly, I've discovered that the most unhappy people in the world are those who use the word *tomorrow* most often. Because of their inability to act, they don't show up for their own lives, and when they finally realize it, they live with regret and its consequences. This is far from the life I desire for you.

Unfortunately, son, you live in culture where "now" is not fast enough. Self-discipline will help you conquer impulsivity and the desire for instant gratification. Those who understand the value of long-term goals are willing to sacrifice something lesser today for something greater tomorrow. But the self-discipline of deferring pleasure requires practice. You must be willing to pay a price today in order to receive the rewards that come tomorrow. Underachievers are at a great disadvantage because they think too much about the pleasure of the current moment, while high achievers dwell on and are motivated by the value of lasting outcomes. With self-discipline, you are choosing the life of a high-achiever.

Matthew 6:21 tells us that when we place value in a future destination, our hearts follow to that place: "For where your treasure is, there your heart will be also" (NIV). Develop the wisdom even now, Mason. Place your treasure where it matters most, and experience the joy that will follow as your heart takes you to your desired goal.

Life will seldom be about what you can't do and more often will be about what you won't do. Learn to distinguish between the two, son, and you'll be light-years ahead of those around you. Learn to engage self-discipline to overcome the "won't," and forge ahead. The feelings will follow, and you'll find yourself on a path to amazing success.

Remember, discipline happens . . . eventually. Either we take the lead and discipline ourselves or life will, at some point, step in and play the role of disciplinarian for us. Choose to take the lead and succeed, my son.

Dad

46

WORSHIP GOD, NOT
THE EARTH

Ty,

It is fashionable today for people to place a big emphasis on nature while diminishing the emphasis on God. I want you to be aware of this cultural dynamic and observe it as you continue to grow up. Throughout our nation, political activists have largely succeeded in removing God from our classrooms, our football stadiums, and our courtrooms. Unfortunately, he's also disappearing from many of our churches. But while our worship may have shifted from God to nature, our need for God has never been greater.

Unfortunately, worshipping our Creator has become passé in many elite circles, while worshipping his creation has accelerated to a passionate, spiritual fervor. Ironically, worship of the creation over the Creator has become the primary religious experience for many people.

Earth worship is a lot like a contemporary version of biblical false idols; earth worship refers to obsessive attention and reverence given to saving the planet, global warming, and the green movement.

What I want you to understand, Ty, is that these issues are far more political than they are scientific or spiritual. You've seen them become entrenched in the educational system during your lifetime. The most fervent voices saying that our planet is at risk are staunch advocates of a big, controlling, government-centered society. The most enthusiastic promoters of green initiatives, coincidentally, have huge financial incentives for advocating and conforming to "earth-saving" programs. As we've joked, what hotel chain wouldn't want to save a few bucks by suggesting we skip having our sheets and towels laundered so the planet can be saved for our grandchildren? It's smart to track the money trail to help clarify motives on issues like this.

You have already experienced this indoctrination firsthand. Under the protective cover of "science," schoolchildren today are coerced into accepting and complying with the climate-change agenda, whether they or their parents desire it or not. To me, the shocking absence of rebuttal experts (though they are plentiful) invited into schools to offer contradictory evidence reveals the true intent of the movement.

Be aware. Do your own research, and draw your own conclusions on this and all issues, especially the controversial ones. Avoid robotic groupthink at all costs. Assess what is bogus, what is exaggerated, and what is legit. As Christians, we should, of course, be faithful stewards of all of our resources, including our natural habitat. But we must remember that God put these natural resources here for our consumption, use, and blessing.

After all, what logic leads people to worship the effect when they could worship the cause? Who would choose to worship the earth when they could worship its Creator?

Do what's right, Ty, and chase the truth, no matter what!

Dad

47

PRETEND EVERYONE
KNOWS MORE

Brooks,

Several years before I was even a teenager, I committed to learning everything I could about the game of baseball. I checked out every book on baseball and read every biography of famous players available at my school's library. With my parent's help, I also periodically cleaned out the baseball section at my local bookstore. This was my idea of summer reading, and I loved it!

The more I read about baseball, the more I wanted to play. And the more I played, the more I wanted to learn about how to play the game even better at the next level. Naturally, one of my summer rituals included attending baseball camp. In July, when I was about twelve, one of the camp coaches asked a series of questions about the fundamentals of this great sport. I answered the first question correctly and then the second. I answered the third question correctly and then the fourth and . . . then he cut me off. "Let someone else answer," he barked. I shut up for a few minutes.

Shortly afterward, the coach pulled me aside and said that he was very impressed with my knowledge, given that I was still very young. And then he warned me, "But don't you ever get impressed with yourself. If you want to be great, then learn all you can, but always pretend that everybody else is smarter than you are . . . especially coaches who were playing baseball before you were born."

That piece of advice changed my perspective, not just for the rest of the camp, and not just for baseball, but permanently, for everything. I started looking at situations with an expectation that a secret lesson or productive technique would be revealed. In conversations, I started listening as though a valuable insight or aha moment was inevitable. Of course, I wasn't perfect with this practice, and it was clearly more difficult to follow when I found the subject matter boring or irrelevant, which, as I've confessed to you before, was a large percentage of the time.

> Laugh a lot

But once I was out of school and able to follow my own path and pursue my own interests, this mind-set started making a huge difference. I realized that every person and every experience was a potential teacher as long as I was a ready student. I realized that both suffering and success added to my wisdom as long as I was engaged and receptive. I realized that both "the smart" and "the stupid" possessed clues that could make me a better and stronger person if I remained curious and open-minded.

Pretending everyone knows more than I do inspired me to start reading biographies and autobiographies of interesting people who have accomplished extraordinary things. But remember, great lessons can be gained from grandparents, friends, neighbors, your younger brother, and even strangers if you look for them. Pretending everyone knows more than I do inspired me to start devouring self-improvement resources including MP3s (they used to be called audio cassettes when I started listening), books, and DVDs.

From faith to fitness to relationships, marriage, parenting, and business, the internet is full of these kinds of virtual semi-nars and digital resources, and they are available inexpensively in comparison to the positive influence they will have on your future. But remember, time-saving and even life-saving insights can come from any source if you look for them.

I know a lot of stuff about a lot of stuff. But I also know I don't know everything about anything, even baseball. And despite outward appearances, no one else does either. The lon-ger I live, the more apparent this reality becomes. It amazes me, though, that some people are turned off or intimidated by learning. Other people are just lazy. This is not for you, son.

Have an inquisitive mind. Learn how to engage with other people's stories and see life from their point of view. You may not agree with everything they believe, but you'll learn how to love people better and you'll grow wiser in the process. God has gifted all of us with unique gifts, talents, and insights, and you are prudent when you learn to stay humbly coachable. After all, in one way or another, everyone knows more than you and every relationship and life circumstance is an opportunity to learn and to grow.

So whether it's the coach with a reputation for being tough or the widow who sits in the pew in front of you in church every Sunday, everybody who crosses your path has the potential to teach you something of value if you're willing to learn. Be happy and thrilled that everyone knows more! Your life will be the richer for it.

Dad

48

CLARIFY YOUR
INTENTIONS

Zach,

You'll carry a huge advantage through life if you first figure out what's important to you and what you want your life to be about. The most successful people I know are unwavering about what they stand for. They're also convicted about what they will not tolerate, both in themselves and in others. Being unclear about your priorities and principles undermines performance and causes conflicts and relationship problems. And unfortunately, most people seldom see their inability to clarify their goals and life principles as the cause of their frustrations.

Winners and wise men know what they want, why they want it, and how they're going to accomplish what they want. In other words, they have goals, motivation, and plans for accomplishing their goals. Read the stories of the most successful people in the world today, and you'll see what I mean. The clearer you become about what you intend to accomplish, the more likely you'll be to succeed at attaining it. Likewise, the vaguer you are in defining what you're pursuing, the more likely you'll be to waste time, misuse resources, and become distracted.

When you spell out your objectives in vivid detail, you increase your awareness, minimize confusion, and eliminate hesitancy. But along with your short-term goals, you also need long-term objectives that drive you toward your life mission. Precisely worded goals will help you achieve your mission because they tell your brain what to notice, what to pay attention to, and in which direction to go.

Misunderstandings and lack of clarity between two people also cause relationship problems. Think about it. When people resolve their conflicts, they typically say something like, "We cleared it up." One person thinks one thing, the other person assumes something else, and the result is a quarrel or disagreement. These kinds of mix-ups happen all the time in all types of relationships: parent-child, teacher-student, coach-player, boyfriend-girlfriend, husband-wife, business partner-business partner, friend-friend, and boss-employee. Reflect on the last argument or disagreement you had. Was a lack of clarity part of the problem?

Most electronic devices come with troubleshooting guides in case the products don't work properly. At the top of the list of potential problems, you can usually read the instructions, "Make sure device is plugged in." Manufacturers have learned that the most common reason their product fails to work is because people don't plug it into a power source. Even though the solution to this simple problem is obvious, it's frequently overlooked. Likewise, when you're clear about what you want, you already have the power supply to achieve your ambition. If you're not making the progress you'd like to be making, recheck your clarity level. If you're unclear about your destination, you'll feel disconnected or unplugged from your source of power. If life came with a trouble-shooting guide for success, "lack of clarity" would be at the top of the list. Underperforming can typically be traced back to confusion or uncertainty about your desired objective.

So how can you find clarity? Ask God to reveal his will for you through your dreams and desires. Pray for guidance before you set your goals and as you're pursuing them. In all your relationships, keep asking for clarity about what to think next, what to say next, and what to do next. Be open and flexible as you move from one chapter of life to the next, but stick to your principles no matter what. Refocus and recalibrate your vision at least every ninety days, and make sure that what really matters stays priority one. If you get off track, go back and check the first item on your troubleshooting guide. You'll be glad you did.

Dad

49

ACT WITH INTELLIGENCE

Dear Ty,

As simple as it sounds on the surface, acting intelligently may be the most challenging habit to practice consistently. This is the habit of thinking, speaking, and behaving in a manner consistent with your desired destination. Since many choices are not preceded by intelligent thought, many actions seem quite foolish. God has blessed you with the faculty of reason for the purpose of taking intelligent action and making wise decisions.

But are you using this faculty?

We live in a world where so many have become educated beyond their intelligence. This means book smart but street foolish, or the absence of good, old-fashioned horse sense. Even more bluntly put, despite our academic credentials, we are all still quite capable of acting like idiots.

So, what will define your intelligence? Is it IQ? Will it be your grade-point average? Will it be the college you attend and the degrees you receive? Maybe it will be your ability to solve problems. Or will it be your ability to develop and maintain healthy, productive relationships? This begs two key questions that are hopelessly interrelated. First, what defines intelligence? Second, what defines stupidity?

As I have devoted most of my adult life to coaching ambitious individuals to reach and exceed their goals, I've developed street-tested definitions of both intelligence and stupidity. Intelligence is a way of acting that moves us closer to the things we value and appreciate in our lives. Stupidity is a way of acting that distances us from the very things we desire and appreciate in our lives.

If my goal is to lose ten pounds, and I sneak brownies into my mouth before I go to bed, I'm an idiot. If your goal is to be an all-state ballplayer, and the only time you hit in the cage is during the team practice, you are an idiot. If I want an awesome relationship with your mom, but I never make time for her, I'm an idiot. If you want to go to a top engineering school but register for the minimum requirement of math classes in high school, you are an idiot. If I want to experience financial freedom, but I sink money into depreciating assets, I'm an idiot. If you want access to the family car, but you give your mom and me a hard time when we ask you to run errands for us . . . you fill in the blank.

What are u living 4?

We all need to acknowledge where we've been idiots. If we don't, there's no end in sight. Every so often we need to think about our goals and just ask ourselves, "How's my current approach working?"

UrbanDictionary.com defines *stupid* as "someone who has to look up 'stupid' in the dictionary because they don't know what it means." Ben Franklin had his own take on it, saying, "We are all born ignorant, but one must work hard to remain stupid."[1]

We have to accept that some people are unwilling or incapable of acting intelligently and therefore cannot be helped. They just have a big case of dumb, or what might be more accurately labeled "inoperable stupidity." Nobel Prize–winning economist

Friedrich Hayek wrote, "We shall not grow wiser before we learn that much that we have done was very foolish."[2] With freedom comes some degree of stupidity, and this goes for individual citizens and the government alike.

There is one big catch to this habit of intelligent action. If we don't know where we are headed, we cannot be certain which road to take or what actions truly are intelligent. Think about how this relates to our country. If we haven't defined what kind of country we want America to be ten, twenty, or thirty years from now, how do we know whether the huge and unprecedented decisions we are making today are wise decisions? If your mom and I haven't defined what kind of life we want to be living in our sixties, then how do we know what we ought to be doing in our forties? If you haven't clarified what you want to be doing when you are twenty-five or thirty, how do you figure out what your top priorities should be as you finish high school and head off to college?

Half of my entrepreneurial clients report being very good students and attending excellent academic colleges. The other half report being average students and attending ordinary colleges. Today, the two groups' income, net worth, health, and overall quality of life seem to be indistinguishable. How is this possible? It's because the second group has mastered the habit of intelligent action.

Son, we are idiots to the degree that we identify a meaningful goal and then think, speak, or act in a manner that moves us further away from that goal. This applies to everyone, from a janitor to a Rhodes scholar. On the flip side, we are geniuses to the degree that we pinpoint a worthy goal and then think, speak, and behave in a manner that moves us closer to that goal. I know what path you're taking, Ty, and I'm very proud of you.

Love,
Dad

50

EXPECT THE BEST

Dear Ty,

Over the next thirty years of your life, you are likely to accomplish many of the goals you set out to achieve. And of course, there will inevitably be some surprises as well. While there are many factors that influence your success, one of the most subtly powerful is your quality of expectation.

Think about it like this. If you want to win, you might win. If you expect to win, you will probably win. If you want her to say yes when you ask her out, she might say yes. If you expect her to say yes, then I'll bet she goes out with you.

I have found that positive expectations and faith are almost the same thing. If you recognize that you want something that you don't now have, then you are off to an okay start. If you expect, at any moment, to receive something that you don't currently have, then you have a running start.

You can distinguish between a want and an expectation fairly easily. If you expect to receive, you get ready to receive. If you *want* to receive, you don't get ready. You just stand there, hoping, but hopeless.

Many times I have texted you and let you know that I had tickets to a ball game or was going to be taking you to dinner that night and asked you to be ready at six thirty when I would pick you up. You had faith, or expected that I would keep my word; you got ready and were waiting for me when I pulled into the driveway. How odd would it have been if you just made other plans and left the house assuming I was going to be a no-show?

Far too many people start down the path toward their goals, son, only to be derailed by weak expectations. They wanted to achieve, but the dominant force of low expectations disrupted their plans.

I don't understand this completely, but I have observed that the quality of our expectations determines the quality of our preparation, which, in turn, determines whether or not we cross the finish line and hit our goals. Remember this: we tend to receive not so much what we want but rather what we expect.

I encourage you to seek the sweet spot where your goals and expectations intersect. Whatever you expect and confidently prepare for tends to show up in your life and often sooner than you could have imagined. It's your optimistic preparation, though, that reveals your true expectation or lack thereof. Frequently, we desire something awesome but get ready for something average.

> U R a winner!

Too often, our best-case scenario is undermined by our own thoughts, words, or behaviors. Too often, we pray for sunshine and then grab our umbrellas.

We should assume great news and think, speak, and act accordingly, with the faith of positive expectations. You can engineer this principle in your favor by preparing as though the realization of your top goal was inevitable and unavoidable, as if it were guaranteed. The very act of getting ready, if we don't feel like it, seems to activate and upgrade our expectations so they start working for us rather than against us.

What kind of life do you want three years from now? Give

this some thought. How about ten years from now? You can achieve far more than you may ever dream of, but only as much as you truly expect.

Expectations cast a vision. In 2008, swimmer Michael Phelps won his seventh gold medal of the games by one-one hundredth of a second when he raised his expectations after he was challenged by a Serbian competitor. Expectations produce hope, and hope is that intangible thing that dreams are made of.

Expect the best of yourself. You're first and foremost a beautiful, wonderful child of God. He has great plans for you—plans that go far beyond what you could dream. Dream big, and have the confidence that God is calling you to something especially with you in mind.

Expect the best of others. The book of 1 Corinthians tells us that love believes all things and bears all things (13:4–7). What you expect of other people will influence how you relate to them. Communicate sincere, positive expectations, and watch as people reflect those expectations in return.

Expect the best of God. At times life will tempt you to despair. But circumstances always point to the reality that we live in a broken world. Trust the love and character of God, who chose to step into the brokenness beside us.

People who focus on gloom and doom see life in a certain way, and their expectations influence their choices and help create a "life-stinks" reality. Your expectations always influence your choices. You can choose to cast a vision for God's best or for something far less.

The choice is yours.

Love,

Dad

51

SIDESTEP THE FAIRNESS CHARADE

Dear Mason,

Can you remember that bratty kid from your childhood who always complained that things were not fair? If he didn't finish his quiz on time, it wasn't fair because of the noise or the lighting, or he didn't feel well, or some other phony reason. If he lost any competition in PE, he'd insist on a do-over or stomp off in a huff.

That obnoxious classmate was right. Life isn't fair.

You've heard me repeat this maxim since you were about two years old. I am not sure why, but children love to complain about things being unfair. Most every parent can attest to this. When little kids and teenagers don't get their way, the reflex response is, "That's not fair." Oddly, in our society today, it is not uncommon to see grown-ups behaving in the same child-ish way. Because of this, I wanted to instill in you, early in your development, the understanding that life is not fair, and not by a long stretch.

The truth is that life, if viewed as a card game, deals good hands, bad hands, and average hands. And whichever hand you receive, you must play! As you know, some people are naturally more intelligent than others. Some people are more creative than others. Some are born into poverty and some into wealth. Some receive great love and little else, while many others are given everything but love.

In your short life, you've no doubt noticed that some people are considered better looking than others. Some people pick up foreign languages or grasp algebra quicker than others. Some people can run faster, jump higher, or throw a football farther than oth-

Make 2day great!

ers. Some have fast metabolisms, while others must exercise twice as much just to keep pace. Some people are predisposed to migraine headaches and sinus infections and others are not. Some receive the best of educations and contribute little to the world, while others get little formal education yet leave an amazing legacy . . . and so on.

By now, you have already started noticing this diverse allocation of gifts and blessings, otherwise referred to as "life." God loves us all equally, and this is why he created us all in his likeness, despite our individual differences. Recognize that everyone has disadvantages, handicaps, weaknesses, and various other crosses to bear. Therefore, a big part of your life will be learning to overcome your disadvantages or even transform them into advantages. This requires plenty of spiritual growth and character development.

Back to the card game. Anyone can win with any hand, and anyone can lose with any hand. It's totally up to the individual and how he chooses to play the game! Life is jam-packed with champions who drew extremely poor hands and with losers who drew terrific hands. I promise you, with God's help, *you can turn any hand you're dealt into a winner.*

One of the great things about America is that no one is born a winner or a loser. We earn this distinction. Losing is not a permanent designation, nor is winning. I know as many losers born into privilege as I do winners born into humble circumstances. While you will run into many who appreciate this truth, you will also have to interact with a large number who are generally oblivious to it.

As I write this letter, there is an animated movement underway attempting to equalize results in America so that no one citizen can do much better than any other citizen. But this kind of fairness, or equalization, ignores the natural order of things. Wherever you look, Mason, you'll find that God's creation yields an inequitable distribution of resources and wealth. Florida has no mountains. Tennessee is ocean challenged. Arizona misses out on the Georgia humidity, and there are no deserts in Pennsylvania. Some countries have greater natural resources than others. While one country has preferable geography, another has a better climate. There is great variety throughout nature, and this is not something that can be "fixed" or "equalized."

Furthermore, our Creator saw fit to bestow personal assets such as talent, creativity, physical strength, physical appearance, intelligence, and other qualities on an unequal basis. This in itself creates so-called unfairness. If you're five foot five and play in the NBA, you're going to have a very unfair experience. If you choose to pursue engineering in college but have difficulty with simple math, your report card and future career will seem quite unfair. If you go into sales but you don't like talking to strangers, your commission checks will reflect some serious inequity. If you possess my singing voice and expect to win *American Idol*, you are going to find the experience outrageously unfair.

I am glad you know that real fairness is when everyone plays by the same rules, enforced by an impartial referee. I am concerned, though, that many in your generation have lost the clear-cut concept of fairness in a gray sea of subjectivity and relativity. The problem is that life is naturally unfair. Liberty breeds inequality—when people are free, those who are smarter, better motivated, and harder-working will achieve more than others. So the only way to ensure this contemporary notion of fairness, or equal outcomes, is to strangle liberty.

Fairness is a pleasant-sounding word, for sure, but it is no substitute for authentic freedom. This includes the freedom to succeed and fail. In school, in sports, and in the free market, the rules should be fair so anyone utilizing his or her talent, work ethic, and resourcefulness has the opportunity to succeed. For example, the punishment for stealing should be the same for the rich, the poor, the pretty, the ugly, the smart, the stupid, the kind, and the rude.

Hitting a baseball prepared me for the reality of American life—I got acclimated to succeeding (getting a hit) only 30 or 40 percent of the time. That prepared me for the inherent inequities of life, as did the pitchers who could throw the ball past me, my opponents who could outrun me, and so on.

I didn't miss a sinking curve ball and complain that it was unfair. Instead, I spent extra time in the batting cage so I would be better prepared the next time. Because of my work ethic, I surpassed many who had more natural talent. Some were better than me, and I accepted that. But I always attempted to get better—I never strove to be just as good as the other players. I worked hard to make sure I outperformed as many teammates and competitors as possible. In other words, I tried to be my best. This didn't make me a better person, just a better player. In fact, I believed in—and still believe in—earned inequality: making yourself better through the persistent application of your God-given talent bank. I want you to do the same.

The most predictable way to make yourself unequal is by the way you lead your life. Obviously, all choices and behaviors are not equal. Making bad choices makes life seem really unfair. Neglecting your health or your studies or your finances can make life seem pretty unfair. Fairness used to mean playing by the same rules and having impartial referees. Today, fairness is evolving into equal outcomes. The truth is that life wasn't designed to be fair. We cannot make life fair. It is both impossible and, upon deeper examination, undesirable. Anyone who loves equality more than freedom is likely to wind up with neither.

Thanks to the grace of God, we can celebrate that life is not fair, and that we won't get what we really deserve. Give this some thought and let's talk about this some more.

Love,
Dad

52

FORGIVE WITH ABANDON

Zach,

The road ahead of you will have its bumps, as well as some jaw-jarring potholes. But no matter how much life may rattle you and people might disappoint you, learn to forgive others.

Forgive everyone, Zach, without exception, for all the crazy, hurtful, and inconsiderate things they may have ever done and will ever do to you. We're all human. Stuff happens. Let it go, move on, and leave it behind.

And since no one is perfect, forgiveness will need to become a lifestyle. Never let old wounds fester by giving them excessive attention. When you carry bitterness, hostility, and emotional baggage, you live in the past and cannot fully realize the joy of the current moment. Your spiritual, mental, and physical health depends upon your ability to become an unstoppable forgiveness machine.

And commit to forgiving yourself, Zach. Learning how to do this can be harder than it sounds. But mastering self-forgiveness holds the key to your spiritual and mental health. It's imperative to learn to forgive yourself without holding back or attaching strings for stupid choices, inappropriate thoughts, limiting words, foolish behaviors, negative beliefs, and other self-defeating choices and attitudes.

Accept God's grace. You have no reason to carry guilt once

you've repented. Jesus paid the price for every silly, stupid, and sinful thing you or anyone has ever done, so accept the peace he offers. God pardoned you. The ultimate act of pride is to say God's forgiveness is sufficient for everyone else, but not for you.

Of course you're not perfect. No one is. But what this means is that you must incorporate self-forgiveness as a lifelong, daily practice; and the sooner you master this skill, the freer you'll be to focus on God's vision and purpose for your life.

Forgiveness frees you in ways that bring growth and maturity, Zach. It breaks the chains that connect you to the hurts of the past, releasing you to focus on the future. It frees you from the emotional burden of bitterness and resentment and makes space in your life for truly important things.

> What's ur dream?

Freedom teaches you the meaning of grace. It makes you more like Jesus as you pass on God's forgiveness to others. Freedom cultivates spiritual perspective, reminding you who you are in relation to God and others.

Years ago it helped me understand that forgiveness doesn't make the other person right; it just keeps me spiritually healthy. Forgiveness is a spiritual discipline that demonstrates your obedience to God. Realize that it is not necessary or even common to feel like forgiving, but do it anyway, just as you would any other requirement of a productive life. While you may not feel awesome ten minutes later or even ten days after, the act of forgiving another person kicks off a chain-reaction of emotional blessings that unfold on God's timetable.

No matter where life takes you, Zach, you are enriched when you know the power of forgiving yourself and others. Live richly, forgive liberally, and enjoy the rewards of the wise, my son.

Dad

53

FILTER YOUR FEELINGS
WITH REASON

Dear Trey,

One of my friends was the victim of a robbery when she was a teenager. After she was married, her husband was very careful to try to make her feel safe. One weekend when he was away traveling, she awoke in the middle of the night to the sound of voices whispering in the bushes beneath her bedroom window. Frightened, she went to a closet and found a weapon, then picked up the phone and called the police.

Within minutes officers arrived and confronted a terrified group of high school students who had been busily at work TPing the house of their high school principal who'd left his wife behind to attend an out-of-state basketball conference.

You and I are wired to respond to emotional triggers in familiar ways. But what we think we see is often an illusion. Trauma, memories, routine, and fear can create emotional mirages that can appear to be remarkably real. What you need to know, son, is that you can never trust your feelings to represent facts and reality. Fear can distort your vision. Pride can corrupt your perception of self and others. Anger can warp your judgment. Love can obscure your reason. In order to trust your perceptions, you must filter your feelings with reason.

Unfortunately, most people believe their feelings are a measurement of reality rather than ever-changing, subjective responses to people, circumstances, and surroundings. One of the most valuable lessons you can learn will be to distinguish between truth and emotion. Learn to value what is true, right, and immovable simply because it is true, not because of the feelings attached to the circumstance. Look to God's Word as your standard for unchanging truth. Culture changes, but truth does not. Opinions change, but truth does not. Learn to distinguish between preferences (opinions), convictions (areas where Scriptural positions vary and you can choose), and nonnegotiables (areas where the Bible takes an unwavering stand). It will be easy to believe what you want to believe if you don't first check your opinions against the Word of God.

Feelings are one of God's most important built-in feedback devices, but feelings will often lead you down a dead-end street. For instance, you will recall that several of your coaches asked you to get up at five in the morning to work out

Pray

before school. You certainly didn't feel like dragging your tail out of bed and into the weight room while it was still dark out and most of your classmates were still asleep. But, you ignored those feelings and instead focused on the goal instead. You had already learned that winners are motivated by fun outcomes and losers are motivated by fun methods. You knew the uncomfortable choice was the best choice for your integrity, for the interests of the team, and for your future.

Feelings can also be deceptive when it comes to relationships with people. You often won't feel like forgiving or going the extra mile or granting people grace. In *Mere Christianity*, C. S. Lewis wrote,

> The rule for all of us is perfectly simple. Do not waste time
> bothering whether you "love" your neighbor; act as if you

did. As soon as we do this, we find one of the great secrets. When you are behaving as if you love someone, you will presently come to love him. If you injure someone you dislike, you will find yourself disliking him more. If you do him a good turn, you will find yourself disliking him less.

You can change your perceptions through your actions, and your heart will follow. This will be an important principle in marriage as well in your relationships on the job.

Son, always filter your feelings first through God's Word, then through the facts, evidence, and background associated with your feelings. Feelings are always subjective and biased, meaning they can and will mislead you. Our culture celebrates empathetic decision making, doing what "feels right," and following your heart. But this approach will almost always lead you into doing things you'll someday regret.

Consider the five decisions from your past you wish you could undo. When you made those decisions, did you first stop to filter them through biblical principles or your long-term goals for your life? Did you consider the facts, the consequences, and the context of your decisions?

Most adults, including me, can look back and recall decisions they regret that "felt right" at the time, as well as smart decisions that didn't feel so right. Even adults have blind spots that can chain us to our feelings, repeating patterns of behavior that hold us back in relationships, careers, and our spiritual lives.

You're not a victim of your emotions. God created you with the power to shape your emotions by the way you choose to think. Your objective is to make sure your emotions don't run the show. How will you do that? Commit to telling yourself the truth, the whole truth, and nothing but the truth, and filter your feelings.

Love you,

Dad

54

CONTEMPLATE GOD'S CHARACTER

Mason,

One of the most powerful habits you can develop early in life is deliberately thinking about God. In particular, I am referring to thinking deeply about the character or nature of our Creator. As you know, *character* is the common word used to describe a person's mental and moral qualities. Our character is the combination of traits that make up the essence of who we are as individuals.

If I asked you to ponder my character, you would consider what you know to be true about me, both good and bad. Because I'm human, my nature is obviously flawed. Since you have lived with me for a number of years, you can confirm this, right?

All kidding aside, despite your respect for me, you know I am not perfect and I possess both weakness and strength. Well, the totality of my virtues and vices is my character. What others believe to be true about me is my reputation, but what God knows to be true about me is my character.

If I asked you to think about the man who lives three houses down from us and you had never met him or heard much about him, it would be a difficult and frustrating task to think about him for very long or in much detail. If I asked you to think about your mom, it would be much easier because you have a relationship with her and have spent a lot of time around her in all kinds of different situations.

Thinking about God is simply thinking about his character, which, in opposition to mine, happens to be perfect. But if you haven't gotten to know God very well, the way you haven't gotten to know the man down the street, you will have some difficulty thinking about him for very long. That scenario would be a real shame. I am only one of millions who can verify that regularly contemplating God produces peace, joy, and often "wow" experiences. Thinking about God's character means thinking about what God is really like. And it does require that you know enough about him to easily run through his qualities in your mind and ponder what they mean to you and what they mean to the world.

Contemplating the nature and character of God is really just a form of prayer. In fact, there is likely no higher plane of thinking than thinking about God. To get started, remember that like any new practice, it may feel awkward at first. Also, there is no right

Believe in yourself!

or wrong way to practice this spiritual discipline, as long as you sincerely desire to be in his presence. You could begin by mentally rehearsing what you know to be true about him. Then challenge yourself to fully understand and appreciate the significance of that quality of God's character.

For example: God is love. What does this mean to you? What does this mean for humanity? God is all-powerful. What is the significance of this to you today and in the future? God is ever present. Then consider the scope and reach of this truth. God is all knowing. Doesn't this mean he has answers for anything you will ever face? God is absolute truth. God is holy. God is merciful. God is faithful. God is just. God is unchanging. Preoccupy yourself in these character qualities of your heavenly Father. Of course, the preceding description is just the beginning.

While God is ever present, you will not necessarily experience his presence unless you reach out to him and acknowledge him with your thoughts. Only when you escape into his presence can you experience permanent fulfillment. The more you practice his presence, the more natural and normal it will become.

Love,
Dad

55

FIGHT AGAINST SOCIALISM

Dear Ty,

The Founders of our nation drew a direct connection between private property, liberty, and the mandates of the Bible. As John Adams wrote, "The moment the idea is admitted into society that property is not as sacred as the laws of God, and that there is not a force of law and public justice to protect it, anarchy and tyranny commence. Property must be secured or liberty cannot exist."[1]

This was a lesson learned in the first moments of American history. The Jamestown colony, established in 1607, initially rejected private property, instead adopting a communal system similar to socialism. Everyone worked the land together and divided up the harvest. As a result, according to colony secretary Ralph Hamor, most of the work was done by one-fifth of the men, the other four-fifths living as freeloaders.[2] Despite fertile soil and abundant game, most of the colonists died of starvation. Chaos emerged, with reports of settlers eating cats, dogs, rats, and even their deceased neighbors. Then the colony converted to private property and it quickly thrived, attracting new settlers from all over Europe.[3] Hamor noted that after the switch there was "plenty of food, which every man by his own industry may easily and doth procure."[4]

A near-identical situation emerged at the Plymouth colony,

which also began with a communal farming system. The governor of the colony, William Bradford, recounted that "young men that are most able and fit for labor and service" protested having to "spend their time and strength to work for other men's wives and children."[5] To correct the terrible situation, Bradford assigned each family their own parcel of land and told them to provide for themselves. And that's exactly what they did. Bradford saw a divine hand in the adoption of private property, relating that "instead of famine, now God gave them plenty."[6] In 1624, there were even enough surpluses to begin exporting corn. Bradford concluded,

> The failure of this experiment of communal service, which was tried for several years, and by good and honest men proves the emptiness of the theory of Plato and other ancients, applauded by some of later times, that the taking away of private property, and the possession of it in community, by a commonwealth, would make a state happy and flourishing; as if it were wiser than God.[7]

Despite these practical lessons as well as biblical teachings, socialism seeks to minimize private property or abolish it altogether. That's because private property spawns competition and inequality, and acts as a check on government control. And keep in mind, private property refers to more than just land. It includes your future home, your car, your cash, and all your other physical possessions.

One of the greatest threats to you and your generation is socialism. For this reason, I want you to know the truth about this philosophy and the worldview that corresponds with it. It has become apparent to me that what is being taught in most schools concerning socialism is as unsettling as it is unsound.

The power teachers, administrators, and textbook publishers have to shape and mold your mind and those of your generation is immense. Only three decades ago I learned the concrete realities of socialism in the classroom during my years of formal education. In most academic circles today, however, it is considered inappropriate to judge one form of government as superior to another. Be aware, though, that socialism is more than just a form of government.

Understand that socialism is predominantly an attitude. We have talked a lot about having a good attitude toward your schoolwork and possessing the right attitude for athletic success, as well as when dealing with difficulty and adversity. Well, people also develop attitudes toward government and freedom. This is what I want to share with you before you become overexposed to the dreamy promises of socialism in your remaining school years and beyond.

To begin, let me give you a mini-lesson. Rooted in the philosophy of collectivism, socialism elevates the needs of the group above the freedom of the individual. Individualism is downplayed or even mocked, and the collective value of particular groups and group effort is emphasized. Pleasant-sounding slogans such as "we're all in this together" and "nobody succeeds on their own" and "mutual responsibility" epitomize this mind-set.

Succinctly, here's how socialism works. In an effort to equalize economic results, the fruit of one person's labor is confiscated and transferred to a fellow citizen considered more deserving in the eyes of the government. Imagine if your principal or academic dean had this kind of power and could transfer some portion of your GPA to one of your classmates at his discretion. Give that some thought. How might GPA redistribution affect your motivation and drive?

Now, let me clarify some semantic confusion that obscures

the truth about socialism. Complete socialism is called communism. Partial communism is called socialism. The difference between the two philosophies is just a matter of degree, or more precisely, a measure of implementation.

> Iron sharpens iron

You can find all sorts of convoluted definitions and descriptions if you do a little research, but the important thing is that you see the big picture. A socialist regime can materialize violently through force or peacefully by popular election and with the degree of socialization fluctuating over time.

In Marx's manifesto, communism is the final stage of socialism, where the government falls away and citizens live together in perfect harmony. In a quick scan of the history books, however, you will not be able to find a single instance of the "government falling away." Socialist regimes have included the Soviet Union, Cuba, North Korea, and Communist China, as well as the gentler social democracies of Western Europe.

Modern socialism is pleasantly labeled "social democracy" and refers to the gradual transition from capitalism to socialism, usually under the authority of distressed and uninformed voters. Casually, and for all intents and purposes, big government and socialism are one and the same. Europe today and the chronic financial malaise of the European Union epitomize the incurable defects of socialistic thinking and governing.

What we call it, though, doesn't matter because more than anything else, socialism reflects a state of mind, a philosophy, and an outlook on life. The British prime minister Winston Churchill described it like this: "Socialism is a philosophy of failure, the creed of ignorance, and the gospel of envy; its inherent virtue is the equal sharing of misery."[8]

The late Baptist pastor Adrian Rogers said it like this:

What one person receives without working for, another person must work for without receiving. The government cannot give to anybody anything that the government does not first take from somebody else. When half of the people get the idea that they do not have to work because the other half is going to take care of them, and when the other half gets the idea that it does no good to work because somebody else is going to get what they work for, that my dear friend, is about the end of any nation. You cannot multiply wealth by dividing it.

Socialism is also an economic system that opposes the free market. In lieu of private ownership, socialism advocates government ownership or partial ownership of production and distribution capability. Today, socialist politicians more often seek control of commerce through regulation than direct ownership, but the impact is nearly identical: economic freedom diminishes, entrepreneurial incentives fade, innovation drops, debt rises, and reliance on government assistance grows.

In the free market, service, competition, and mutual self-interest drive the economy. Buyer and seller trade goods or services for the mutual benefit of both parties and with the intent of maintaining a voluntary but jointly beneficial long-term relationship.

Socialism is also a political order that concentrates wealth in the hands of an "elite" group of government officials who portend to redistribute that wealth in a manner they deem to be fair or equitable. Ironically, socialists complain about the dangers of having too much wealth concentrated in the hands of a few private individuals who actually earned it, when socialism simply transfers and then concentrates wealth in the hands of a few politicians who had no role in earning it.

Ty, which scenario are you more comfortable with?

Finally, socialism is a secular philosophy that contradicts scriptural truth. The process of socialization is virtually always preceded by secularization. Over the last few decades, as America has drifted away from God, we have drifted toward socialism as well. As God fades from our attention, so does liberty. Evil in all its varieties is just the natural outgrowth of freedom without God. You can review the whole history of socialism as well as fascism and see for yourself that nothing good came from it.

So that we could better grasp his love for us and the cherished connection he desires to have with us, God established the father-child relationship theme beginning in Genesis and running throughout the Bible. To fully appreciate the incompatibility of socialism with biblical truth, we should understand how this spiritual metaphor reinforces our correct standing with God.

Let me explain. There are many ways we can imitate our heavenly father. We imitate God when we tell the truth, when we act in love, when we show grace, when we are faithful to our spouses, when we are wise stewards of our resources, when we are industrious, when we demonstrate faith, and so on. When we copy God's ways, we reflect his character in our lives. As the apostle Paul said, "Be imitators of God, therefore, as dearly loved children" (Eph. 5:1 NIV).

We imitate God when we are productive human beings, when we employ our natural gifts, and when we encourage others, especially our children, to do likewise. When God created you and me, he planted within us the instinct and drive to work, invent, produce, create, and own, because in doing so, we imitate him, assign credit to him, and further his creation.

A natural validation of biblical truth, capitalism brings out all these qualities of character that God wants to develop within us. To succeed in the free market, we have to be creative, service minded, generous, industrious, self-reliant, frugal, and resourceful. Whether we are a small-business owner, plumber, banker, or chief executive, capitalism is all about learning from our mistakes, overcoming fear, and serving others in ways that are desired, appreciated, and rewarded.

Socialism limits freedom, depresses excellence, and rewards mediocrity. Socialist practices put arbitrary and artificial limits on personal ambition, suffocating the divine spark of innovation that has historically increased prosperity for millions—and will continue to do so if it's not snuffed out in the near or distant future.

Socialism is about dependence on government. The Bible is about dependence on God.

This is a battle worth fighting, and I encourage you to lead the way.

Love,

Dad

56

CULTIVATE LIFELONG INTEGRITY

Dear Brooks,

Long before you were born, I heard Hall of Fame college football coach Lou Holtz recite these words on stage, and I have never forgotten them:

> You got it from your father; maybe it was all he had to give.
> Now it's yours to use and cherish for as long as you may live.
> You may lose some things he gave you, but they can always
> be replaced, but a black mark on your name, son, can never
> be erased. So guard it very carefully, for when all is said and
> done, you'll be glad the name is spotless when you give it to
> your son.[1]

Integrity, Brooks, is one of those all-or-nothing qualities. You either have it or you don't. The very definition of *integrity* means living by your convictions because they're just that—convictions. People of integrity are willing to stake their lives on what they believe, no matter what. They don't abandon their principles, even if sticking to them means inconvenience, discomfort, unpopularity, or disadvantage. In fact, people who claim to have integrity but cash in their principles for the sake of circumstances or convenience never possessed integrity in the first place.

Integrity is the DNA of your character; it defines the kind of person you are at your core. You wear your integrity like a suit of clothes; the kind of person you are on the inside is the first thing people see represented in the words you say and don't say, and the things you do on the outside. But integrity also shows up in the choices we make when no one is watching. Dwight Moody said, "Character is what you are in the dark."[2]

Because integrity flows from convictions, people with integrity have an easier time discerning right from wrong and making choices. The term itself means "complete and structurally sound" and implies that you're secure and comfortable in your own skin. People with integrity can relax and let their true character shine. They don't have to exaggerate, entertain, distort, disguise, misrepresent, manipulate, hide, or hedge the truth. As one of my mentors told me, "Every addition to the truth is a subtraction from it."

Living with integrity is like living with the security of money in the bank. You know you have the resources you need at your disposal for day-to-day living or the challenging surprises of life. The reverse is true for the person who lacks integrity. When life's challenges come, they find themselves bankrupt in moral character and often make decisions that result in devastating long-term consequences. Young men with high character give up personal gain of any kind to keep their integrity. Whatever the price your integrity demands, pay it and know that you've made a wise investment.

The enemies of integrity are the twin villains of compromise and conformity. Conceding our standards to conform to the opinions of the majority or to compromise with the voices of the popular often seems like the clever, reasonable thing to do.

However, bending the truth is never right and diminishes not only our self-worth but our discernment. Each compromise makes the next one easier, until our integrity erodes and disappears.

What's frightening is that the greatest examples of compromise and conformity that can be seen today are in our nation's political arena. Deception is not only tolerated, it's applauded when it's successful. Anything goes when the ends justify the means. Spin doctors are masters of the tools of deceit: word games, half-truths, and reinventions of the past designed to confuse honest citizens attempting to understand the truth about policies, actions, fiscal spending, and the course of the nation. Leaders of integrity do not focus only on winning and leading; they focus on how they win and how they lead.

Never allow your end goal to obscure the means to your objective, son. Who you are determines where you go and what you will accomplish. The call of integrity is not a call to perfection but a call to inward character that will drive your direction. Focus first on integrity, and the other issues of life will naturally fall into place.

> Smile—God loves u always and forever

Love,
Dad

57

EXPERIENCE GOD'S GRACE

Zach,

    I've always admired heroes who helped shape our nation, especially those who battled to make our nation great. At the end of the Civil War in April of 1865, General Robert E. Lee rode away from his Confederate troops and toward Appomattox, where he surrendered to the commander of the Union Army, General Ulysses S. Grant. Lee was certain he and his men were soon to be imprisoned and that he would be tried and executed. So he was shocked when Grant told him that he and his men were free to return to their homes. Lee offered his sword as a symbol of surrender, but Grant refused it. Humbled, Lee rode away. But in a final act of grace, General Grant took off his hat and offered a parting salute. His compassion left a mark on Robert E. Lee for the rest of his life.[1]

    Grace is an intangible gift that can take your breath away. It offers honor when it's least expected and has not been earned. It offers mercy in place of judgment and pardon in place of penalty. When you experience grace, you get something you don't deserve. Grace is commitment and unconditional acceptance without the requirement of commitment in return. The greatest gift of grace you can possibly receive is the gift of salvation available to all people who deserve to pay the price for the wrong they've done.

Experiencing God's grace means understanding you cannot possibly do enough or work hard enough to pay your way into God's favor. He simply grants you grace, based on the gift of love Jesus paid on your behalf. Understanding grace means you're secure in your relationship with God. He honors you not because of what you've done or what you deserve—because as a sinner you deserve nothing—but because he offers grace as a free gift.

Living with an understanding of grace releases you to live in freedom. Grace means you're accepted. Grace allows you to live without shame. Grace promises God's unconditional commitment. Grace is your seal of security.

Grace is a foreign concept in today's world. Nobody can understand a relationship where a spouse would stick it out with someone who repeatedly walked away from him into the arms of somebody else. But that's exactly what God promises us. That's the wonder of his grace and the difference between being loved by the true God and a false god.

You are the recipient of God's grace, son. Live with a constant awareness and gratitude for that grace. Share this grace with others. And may it draw you closer to the heart of God and his great love for you.

Dad

58

TRAIN FOR ADVERSITY

Dear Ty,

One hot summer day in rural South Georgia, Scott and his college friends went for a ride in the back of a pickup truck. All was fine when suddenly an 18-wheeler careened into the side of the truck, tossing him from the cab to underneath the three-ton attached trailer and dragging him for more than three hundred feet. Waking up in the hospital, Scott Rigsby learned he had suffered third-degree burns, a severed right leg, and an almost detached left leg. Months and then years passed with twenty-six surgeries accompanied by alcohol and prescription drug abuse. With no income, no dreams, and no prospects for a better future, it became a fifteen-year downward spiral. Ultimately, Scott asked doctors to amputate his remaining leg to relieve his pain. It became a turning point.

No longer feeling sorry for himself, and now with two prosthetic legs, Scott heard God's call to make a difference. At that very moment, he made a pledge to break down barriers for physically challenged athletes. He completed thirteen triathlons and five road races on his way to setting world records for a double below-the-knee amputee in the full marathon, half Ironman, and international distance triathlon, earning him a spot on the 2006 USA triathlon team. As his accomplishments mounted, so did Rigsby's desire to do the unthinkable and take his mission to the next level.

And on October 13, 2007, after enduring the elements for sixteen hours and forty-three minutes, Scott Rigsby became the first double-amputee on prosthetics in the world to finish an Ironman distance triathlon at the 140.6-mile World Championship in Kailua-Kona, Hawaii.

Over the years, you've watched me—in the good times and the bad. You've observed how I've responded in the moments when things have gone my way and when I haven't gotten what I thought I deserved out of life. You've seen me in my less-than-happy moments, for instance, when people cut me off in traffic or are rude to your mother, or the day my computer system failed and sent viruses to all my clients. You know that no matter how much I talk about success, I still have to deal with the tough realities of life, like everybody else.

You know, more than anyone, that I'm not perfect. And I hope that in my imperfection I've taught you how to respond to adversity. We all face adversity in life. Sometimes those moments will be public, and crowds will be there to watch us respond as life hurls obstacles, disappointments, and heartbreak in our direction. And sometimes our struggles with adversity will be private, and we'll face our battles behind closed doors or in the sheltering presence of those we love.

The question is never whether or not adversity will come but *when* it will come and how you will choose to respond to it. We live in a world of defective people, Ty. That means you and me too. No matter how good our intentions may be, it's unrealistic to think we won't experience the consequences of living in this imperfect world. Sooner or later, loved ones will die, dreams will be delayed, and relationships will disappoint. Quite simply, life is difficult.

The good news is that God, in his goodness and grace, has made it possible for adversity to work for our good. He promises to use even the pain of life not only to shape and mold our characters but to bring about good that exceeds our understanding. This is why, as Christians, we can "count it all joy" (James 1:2 NKJV) when we face difficult and sometimes just plain gut-wrenching circumstances.

In the end, wealth is nothing, Ty. Fame is nothing. Position is nothing. The character God grows in us is everything, and he promises he can use adversity to grow us—if we let him. Character develops as we swim against the currents of challenge, change, and conflict. But too many people give in to the pull of the struggle, never tasting victory because they fail to understand that God's greatest gift to us is the freedom and power to change.

Adversity will come to you in life in all shapes and sizes and with assorted labels: hardship, crisis, difficulty, challenge, setback, failure, and suffering. At one point or another, it may strike your physical body, your marriage, your family, your finances, or any other corner of your life. And each and every trial will be a chisel that can shape the possibilities within your character.

As strange as it may sound, I encourage you to welcome adversity, son, because it will introduce you to the possibilities within yourself. God allows it to be a portal to new learning, new insight, new ministry, new relationships, and new potential. Adversity isn't pleasant, but if it didn't take us to places that stripped us of the self-reliance we draw from ambition, pride, wealth, success, and fame, it could not do its work.

> Forgive someone

When you see adversity as a strength builder, you weaken its negative energy. When you understand it's an ally and a necessary part of growth, you're able to see the possibilities that lie in the challenges in your path. Sometimes you'll face adversity because of your own stupidity. This kind of trial comes when you've been thoughtless or reckless—sometimes in decisions you've forgotten about long ago—and you eventually reap the consequences.

At other times you'll face what I call tragic adversity that comes from unpredictable and inevitable crises in life that rock your world. These kinds of traumas often come without warning and strike those you love. They will either strengthen you or break you. You will feel out of control, and prayer and faith will often be your only recourse. Your responses, however, will be within your control and will shape who you will become.

Bold adversity comes when you pursue demanding goals that place you in the top tier of risk takers. This type of adversity includes facing loneliness because the ranks of those who attempt huge goals are never crowded. And while the views are magnificent, the price of the entry ticket is expensive. Huge goals bring about huge obstacles and, ultimately, huge rewards. When you attempt hard things, you will face hard resistance. Confronting adversity head-on as you pursue audacious goals requires *ambition*—sometimes an unpopular word—as well as initiative and self-confidence. But the reward is achieving your fullest God-given potential.

I see the potential within you, son. Don't see adversity as a threat to the great things that lie ahead but rather as part of the training that will strengthen and equip you. Know most of all that I'm proud of you and standing beside you all the way.

Love,
Dad

59

LAUGH AT POLITICAL CORRECTNESS

Trey,

Abraham Lincoln was once arguing a point with his cabinet minister, Edwin Stanton. He stopped the conversation and asked, "If you call a dog's tail a leg, how many legs would the dog now have?"

Stanton quickly replied, "Five."

"No," replied Lincoln. "Calling a dog's tail a leg doesn't make it a leg."

The point seems obvious. Calling something by a different name doesn't change what it really is. But this is exactly the bait and switch we're seeing in popular culture—in our government, the media, our educational system, scientific circles, and the corporate workplace. It's called "political correctness," and it's the five-legged dog that's wagging the tail of America.

Political correctness is quickly altering

our culture from the inside out. Even citizens who are pretty sure they're looking at a four-legged dog apologize sheepishly and parrot the popular party line. Censorship has become the new American standard. All opinions are created equal unless the topics under discussion turn to traditional religious and moral values. Citizens by the thousands are being forced to surrender their freedom of thought, speech, and expression.

Political correctness has us turning inside-out in futile efforts to be inoffensive. Schools can no longer celebrate Mother's Day because some kids don't have moms. And Father's Day is out the door too. Some schools have banned boys' bathrooms and girls' bathrooms, claiming unisex facilities are the only equitable way to go (no pun intended, well . . . maybe).

The very definition of *holiday* assumes tradition and, hold your breath here, our distinctiveness. St. Patrick's Day is pretty much for the Irish. Mother's Day is about moms. Christmas is about Christ. Hanukah is for Jews. Veterans' Day is for veterans. Perhaps we need to ban that, too, for fear of conscientious objections from conscientious objectors. Take the arguments of political correctness to their logical conclusion, and America becomes one massive lump of sameness.

And the silliness continues as we reinvent our vocabulary in a vain effort to be inoffensive to everyone. The PC dictionary police now demand that we remove words as often as we take out the trash. Gender neutrality has wiped out a long and ever-growing list of terms. *Flight attendant* replaced *stewardess*. *Waiters* and *waitresses* became servers. *Firemen* became firepersons and then *firefighters*. The PC police scratched their heads a bit over *freshmen* before they came up with the tongue-twisting *incoming first-year students*. Eighteen-year-olds all over the nation heaved a sigh as they were overwhelmed with an increased sense of personhood.

We don't need government to label its citizens and censor language in an effort to re-create reality. Our government's desire to be politically correct is a lost cause in a culture where the word *correct* is denied a clear moral foundation.

As Americans, our job is to know truth, recognize truth, integrate truth in life, and become the gatekeepers of truth for future generations. Political correctness, at its core, is deception and a shell game. Don't buy it, son. Look at the dog. A leg will always be a leg, and a tail will always be a tail.

Dad

60

DEBRIEF AND REFLECT

Dear Ty,

Do you remember the car rides home after Little League baseball? With Slush Puppie in hand, I'd ask you three quick questions. First, "What did you like about the way you played?" Then, "What didn't you like about your performance?" Finally, I'd ask, "If you could replay the game, what would you do differently?"

Sometimes I would ask you a few follow-up questions, and other times your answers were so thorough that no follow-up was necessary. Within a couple of minutes, we were done and already talking about other non-baseball stuff long before we arrived back at home.

At the time, you didn't necessarily know that we were debriefing your game together, and, in particular, how well you played. While I certainly hoped the short exercise would help you play better the next game, my real motive was to get you into the habit of evaluating yourself honestly and objectively for the purpose of continuous improvement, not just in baseball, of course, but in all of life for the rest of your life.

Go 4 it!

Debriefing is a term that originated with the military. When fighter pilots and other soldiers returned from missions, they would be interviewed and asked a series of questions by their superiors to figure out what they had learned and what enemy intelligence had been obtained. The objective was to incorporate what had been uncovered into the overall battle plan, as well as to share this new information with other personnel before they launched their own missions.

Reflecting is a very similar term to *debriefing*. And it is just what it sounds like—looking back. But it's more than that. It's the ability to see important lessons in the past that will help you make better decisions in the present that will influence your future results.

Grown-ups and teenagers alike live at a crazy pace today, and far too few people carve out time to regularly evaluate their decisions and assess the direction of their lives. This is what debriefing and reflection are all about. Even fewer people create plans for their futures. Most Americans simply allow themselves to be swept along in a current of frenzied activity, consoling themselves that an overloaded calendar is a sign of success.

As a result of our superficial focus, we develop blind spots, miss breakthrough opportunities, neglect relationships, and repeat the mistakes of our pasts. We overlook the valuable tools of reflection and introspection and only turn to them in times of crisis or tragedy. But reflection will be most valuable to you, son, when it becomes part of the fabric of your life—when you leverage it to help you see possibilities, avoid pitfalls, and create sustained, positive momentum.

One of our best etched memories came from my friend and longtime coaching client Mike Campbell. As a former member of the Blue Angels, Mr. Campbell set us up with front-row tickets and even secured tarmac passes allowing for our once-in-a-lifetime experience to be captured in a very cool photograph in front of the blue jets.

Needless to say, the navy's Blue Angels inspired and created a "wow" experience for all of us. Their commitment to excellence is simply remarkable, and it's demonstrated in all they do. But their success rests, in part, upon their practice of regular reflection. After every show, the team debriefs to evaluate, course correct, and make adjustments before their next performance. Team members watch videos to look for what went right and what went wrong, and they address errors with the language of personal responsibility: "I'll fix it."

Ty, you'll stand among the ranks of the wise if you too can learn to evaluate, course correct, and make adjustments as part of the discipline of your life. As your father, I want to pass on skills that will help you become a godly man, a peak performer, and an influential leader. And while I don't claim to know everything, I've been blessed with opportunities and relationships that have helped me understand the way people learn, think, and grow. Lessons from my own reflection are part of my legacy to you.

In the years ahead, you'll be challenged by unexpected losses and exhilarating successes. But whether you process those experiences as successes or failures will rest in your ability to reflect upon them and use them. Debriefing and reflecting have been very helpful to both my business and personal growth.

And the simple process begins with just a few key questions, not unlike the ones I first shared with you during your years of Little League baseball. Essentially, reflection requires very little time, but a decent amount of thought.

You begin by hitting the pause button on your physical and mental activity so you can think clearly. Once you are still and undistracted, hit the rewind button. This means glancing back in the rearview mirror and studying the situations, relationships, and events that cannot be changed, whether positive or negative, awesome or awful. Ask yourself, "What went well in this circumstance, class, game, or phase of life?"

Then, ask yourself, "What didn't work, and what was my contribution to the situation?" Be willing to acknowledge where you're missing the mark and to identify weak spots so you can correct them before you're left with damaging consequences, negative thought patterns, or default behaviors.

Finally, hit the fast-forward button on your life. Ask yourself, "What do I need to do differently or improve about myself before the next game, the next exam, the next relationship, or the next interview?" You have the power to translate the work of reflection into positive change. Ask questions that will move you forward: "How can I modify my strategy and change my approach so I can perform better in the future? How can I leverage my strengths? How can I manage my weaknesses?" My best clients do this drill weekly, and a few even do an abbreviated version in the evening and after every important business or personal activity.

Son, the practice of reflection combined with debriefing the significant moments of your life will serve you well at all times, in all seasons, and in all circumstances of life. Reflection will reap a reward in your personal life, professional life, and spiritual life. When you think proactively and reflectively, you will gain key opportunities for growth.

Proverbs 14:8 sums up my heart for you as a father: "The wisdom of the prudent is to give thought to their ways" (NIV). May you continue to grow in godly wisdom, Ty.

Love,

Dad

61

AVOID VICTIMITIS

Dear Zach,

Show me someone with a victim mind-set and I'll show you someone stuck in mediocrity. Victimhood is groupthink. It's an attitude of helplessness and hopelessness that expends its efforts in wasted activism rather than productive efforts. And unfortunately, victimitis, or the uncontrolled inflammation of the gripe gland, has spread like the swine flu through our land. For example, Charles Sykes, author of *A Nation of Victims*, points out that if we added up all the groups who consider themselves to be victims or oppressed, their number would total almost 400 percent of America's population. I am not sure whether to laugh or cry at this statistic.

And for most of us, listening to the whine of chronic victims has become exhausting. Victims use guilt and manipulation as ways of making others feel guilty about the positive things in their lives. People with victimitis shut down honest channels for living with dignity and integrity. Because manipulation and negativity undermine trust, victims sabotage efforts for their legitimate gripes to be heard.

Of course, true victims do exist, and it's pretty easy to spot them among the phonies. A wife and young mother loses her husband, a fallen police officer. A tornado decimates a family.

Anguished parents return to an empty house after burying their teenage son. A seven-year-old boy fights cancer. A teenage girl sets aside dreams of dancing as she's fitted for a wheelchair. Night after night we see victims of violent crime. And even though the years have passed, we still remember the faces of September 11 and the families left behind.

You know true victims and the hardships they endure. You know people who've lost loved ones to disease or sudden death and have never recovered or gotten over it. But they learn to deal with their losses over time, and they refuse to let the pain define them. What's interesting, Zach, is that true victims seldom see themselves as victims at all. Grace in the face of pain draws love, support, and generosity.

Victimitis, however, wears a different face. Victims proudly wear labels in order to draw attention to themselves and to gain an advantage over other people. Victims live in the past and replay their hurts like cable-TV reruns. They see themselves as wronged and nurse old wounds. They're not responsible for anything because everything is someone else's fault. Their character slowly rots as they sit and soak in a sour past.

Legendary basketball coach John Wooden said, "Don't let what you cannot do interfere with what you can do."[1] Victims turn this advice on its head. They focus on the fact that they're not succeeding rather than on ways they could. They define them-selves by their deficiencies and inadequacies, so their thinking becomes limited by what they can't do rather than expanded by what they can do. Their thinking teaches them how to be helpless and is a prescription for a mediocre life, not because these people are victims, but because they choose victim as their primary identity.

> Think huge!

The goal of those infected with victimitis is to avoid the

responsibilities and consequences of their choices. Victims blame others. They claim moral superiority while they refuse personal responsibility. Victims say they're looking for justice and fairness, but their words are hollow since they insist on being right and entitled to sympathy.

The life of a victim isn't the life I want for you, Zach. I want you to focus on your potential, not your past. I want you to build a future, not wallow in a warped version of history. I want you to reflect your heritage. Americans are the most compassionate people in the world. We show compassion for our families and communities by taking care of ourselves, and we take care of our families, our friends, and our neighbors. We love helping others, especially when they're in need.

But our political leaders hunt for fresh victims to spoil— especially in a fragile economy. Victims can only be helped temporarily before they fall back into their old patterns of thinking. Complaints create more opportunities to "fix injustice," and the cycle of victimitis continues. And as the cycle continues, the responsible lose more freedom.

My prayer is for you to be a victor, not a victim, Zach. For you to be a man who builds instead of tearing down. Who takes responsibility instead of pointing fingers. Who pitches in instead of sitting on the sidelines. Who makes a change instead of making excuses. Resist victimitis, Zach. It's a war worth fighting—personally and for the sake of our nation.

Love,

Dad

62

AFTER YOU SCREW UP, STEP UP

Brooks,

We all screw up; it is inevitable. Once you realize that it is a matter of "when" and not "if" you are going to make mistakes, then you will know that your response can make you or break you. When you make a big mistake or get caught in a big sin and have to face the consequences, I pray that those poor choices only create short-term pain and do not cost a life, a dream, or a close relationship. If you are fortunate, you may experience the negative repercussions as a rather private matter. But there is no assurance of this. Today, very few of our transgressions remain private or off limits to the rest of the world.

Remember, you are not going to face self-inflicted turmoil because you are a necessarily "bad person." You will sooner or later screw up entirely because you are human. Of course, it is always useful to examine one's character and try to uncover any potential blind spots or weak spots following getting into trouble of any kind. And when you face adversity brought about by your own foolish choices, I want you to remember these four things:

- God still loves you the same as before and always
- Your mom and I love you no matter what
- You can and will bounce back if you keep your faith in God and His Word.
- Learn from your mistakes so you don't make them over and over again.

Believe it or not, it's a blessing to be caught early when you are violating God's principles and compromising your own values system. No doubt that it is okay and natural to not feel good, much less grateful if you've caught. Ha Ha! Nevertheless, thank God anyway! Thank your heavenly father that your wrong behavior has been brought to light, and be grateful for both his grace and mercy — whether you feel like it or not. Allow God to shine light on things He wants to expose, have you learn from them, and put them behind you.

Even if an unacceptable behavior hasn't

become public, own the unwise choice or choices and boldly verbalize 100 percent responsibility for your part in the mess, whatever that might be. Accept the responsibility for what you thought, said, did, or neglected to do that has created these negative conditions in your life. Many of the mistakes you make while young you will laugh about later. Therefore, as appropriate, laugh a good bit right now. There is little to be gained from making mountains out of mole hills. Besides, others in authority will quite likely do that for you anyway. What's done is done. Keep the big picture in mind. It's what you do next that really matters and can lead to maturity and wisdom. Ironically, unwise choices can lead to wisdom, but there is no guarantee that this will be the case. It's up to you. I believe in you and know that the problems you will face are small compared to the resolve in you and God walking beside you.

Your mom and I are continuously praying for your protection, your peers, and your purpose, that nothing would interrupt or sidetrack God's plan for your life. He has such great plans for you. Know that I am in your corner. Like your heavenly father, I am pulling for you and cheering for you even when we are miles apart. Along with your mom, I am ready to help whatever the circumstances may be. You can count on that!

Learn this special verse, Brooks, and keep it handy . . . just in case: "[B]ut one thing [I do], forgetting those things which are behind and reaching forward to those things which are ahead, I press toward the goal for the prize of the upward call of God in Christ Jesus" (Phil. 3:13–14 NKJV).

Dad

63

VISUALIZE GOD'S BLESSINGS

Dear Trey,

You've been taught all your life that you're created in God's image. All humans have unique capabilities distinctive from any other creatures. One of our gifts is the ability to envision a better future than the one we're living. This gift keeps prisoners of war alive in the bleakest of circumstances. It gives a mother hope when her child is diagnosed with a life-threatening illness. It infuses our hope and has given men and women the vision throughout history to pray for dreams that lie beyond present reality.

Prayers are God's most powerful demonstration of our unique ability to envision a better future. It would be unthinkable for people to pray for something less than what they experience in the present. We always pray for something better because God created us with the power to visualize something beyond what presently exists. He's given us the power to visualize so that we can achieve things that surpass present reality, through his power. But surprisingly, most people live their lives visualizing only what they already have. This is a simple yet staggering truth—so staggering that I'll repeat it. God's given us the power to visualize a better future, yet too often we only visualize the things we already have.

But here's the reality, son. You can achieve only what you

reach for. As long as you visualize what you already have, which is our natural human tendency, you'll end up with just that—what you already have. In the Old Testament, God tells his people that "where there is no vision, the people perish" (Prov. 29:18 KJV). This is true of civilizations, businesses, and individuals. When you lose a vision for dreams beyond the status quo, you begin to die on the inside. You lose the vitality and enthusiasm God intended all his children to experience.

The power to visualize is *in* you, but not *of* you. It's a God-given gift with God-given potential. It can be used, abused, or neglected, and the choice is yours. If you're willing to train your mind, you can better prepare yourself to carry out the work God's called you to do. And here's how:

First, visualization requires *deliberation*. Feed your mind vivid pictures of the person God wants you to become. Set aside a portion of each day to visualize yourself in detail performing at your very best—at work, with your spouse or children, or in a sporting event. Visualization works because it relies on the brain's tendency to carry out its most dominant thought. The subconscious mind cannot distinguish between a real and an imagined event, so it processes a goal as if it were already achieved. It interprets visualizations as facts and responds accordingly, removing mental roadblocks or "every high thing," as Paul refers to them, along the way (2 Cor. 10:5 NKJV).

As a Christian, you're told to "set your affection on things above"(Col. 3:2 KJV). Philippians 4:8 tells you to envision things that are true, noble, right, pure, lovely, admirable, excellent, and praiseworthy. Therefore, you should constantly feed your mind with the multisensory images of the end results you hope to achieve. These images command your brain to reproduce the goal of your affections. And the best time to practice this discipline is

> Lead others

before you go to sleep and just after you awake. Relax, step into your own God-prompted movie, and envision the things you see yourself doing as if your prayers were answered and your goals were accomplished. Imagine the outcomes you desire, engage your emotions, and involve as many senses as possible in the process. Persist in envisioning the life you desire, and that image can become reality.

I encourage you to put this advice into action, son. The next time you're praying about a problem, challenge, or issue facing you, take a few extra minutes to relax before you pray. Take a few slow, deep breaths, and imagine your mind free of restraining opinions, preconceived notions, and negative attitudes. Ask God to fill your mind with his wisdom. Affirm that you're open and receptive to God's inspiration and direction. Then visualize Jesus sitting next to you, teaching and advising you. Receive his guidance, and meditate on his love and peace. Thank God for his perfect solution. Experience the confidence of hearing from Jesus in a personal encounter.

The truth is, son, he's waiting for you every day, waiting to share a vision of your future if you'll only take the time to come.

Love,
Dad

64

EVERYTHING COUNTS

Mason,

Early in my business career, one of my mentors shared with me two very important words. These words were *everything counts!* I didn't fully appreciate what it meant at the time, but looking back, I view these two words as some of the best advice I've ever received.

I love the bluntness of this simple truth. It doesn't suggest that some things or many things or even most things count. Quite succinctly, it reminds us that *everything* counts. Not only does today matter, but every moment within this day is important and generates its own future consequences of some kind or another.

As you continue to mature and grow into adulthood, I want you to remember that unlike lacrosse, football, and most other sports, there are no time-outs in life. The game clock is forever ticking, and there are no pause buttons or dress rehearsals either. Consider what this means for your future.

What you think matters. What you say matters. What you mumble to yourself matters. What you do with your time matters. What you read, surf, watch, and repeatedly listen to matters. What you eat and drink matters. What you *don't* eat and drink matters. When you go to sleep and when you wake up matters. How you dress and present yourself to others matters. Even, and especially, the friends you choose to hang out with matter. It's scary but true. There is no place to hide. This is true in sports, relationships, business, family, and finances. It all matters. If you understand, you will instantly become part of the well-informed minority.

A lot of people will scoff at this notion, preferring instead to pretend that certain moments, certain choices, and certain behaviors are neutral and have no real impact on who you become or how your character evolves. What you do Friday night counts, just as what you do Sunday morning or Thursday afternoon counts. Stay alert, as cultural influences will cleverly convince us to sell the future for the present.

This note isn't intended to make you an

uptight and anxious stick-in-the-mud. To the contrary, I want you to have fun, appreciate spontaneity, and experience carefreeness. I am exposing you to this truth so you will organize your hopes and dreams, in fact, your entire life, around it. I want you to become smart enough to *consistently* make smart choices, knowing that both actions and inactions eventually produce matching consequences.

Dad

CONVERSATION STARTERS

LESSON 1

DAD: Describe a few moments in your life when you acted with courage, even though you were afraid or uncomfortable.

SON: What is the most courageous thing you've ever done or wish you had done if you had it to do over?

LESSON 2

DAD: What are two habits you practice that help you manage your time more effectively?

SON: How do you know if you are wasting your time or using it wisely?

LESSON 3

DAD: Who are three successful people you admire and respect, and why?

SON: Who are three successful peers and one other successful individual you respect, and why?

LESSON 4

DAD: What are three big blessings and three tiny blessings you are grateful for, and how do you show your appreciation?

SON: In what ways do you or could you express gratitude for the important relationships in your life?

LESSON 5

DAD: What are three or four of the most life-shaping decisions you've made, and what would you do differently if you had them to do over again?

SON: What are one or two big decisions you've already made and what are the three really big decisions you are likely to make before age thirty?

LESSON 6

DAD: In what ways are the fundamentals of your favorite sport similar to the fundamentals of life?

SON: What is a principle and how is it different from an opinion, theory, or fad?

LESSON 7

DAD: What do you see when you picture yourself and your life ten years into the future?

SON: What kind of images might symbolize your life ten years from now?

LESSON 8

DAD: What makes America a distinctly special place to live?

SON: What have you learned about the American Dream in school?

LESSON 9

DAD: What is the difference between working hard and working smart?

SON: Why is it important to work hard when you are young?

LESSON 10

DAD: What are the things you do regularly that demonstrate God is your number one priority?

SON: How could you start the day with God each morning?

LESSON 11

DAD: What has been you method for determining True North when making important decisions?

SON: How do you distinguish right from wrong?

LESSON 12

DAD: In what areas of your life have you been more likely to assume the gift is hidden, and why?

SON: What's one positive example and one not so positive example of how you responded to bad news or disappointment?

LESSON 13

DAD: Share some of the step-by-step plans you have for your career, finances, fitness, or any other area of life.

SON: Why are you likely to achieve more of the things you want in life if you learn how to plan?

LESSON 14

DAD: In what ways is the Bible like a love letter from a father to his children?

SON: What are some of the questions you ask yourself when you are reading the Bible?

LESSON 15

DAD: If you could relive your life up to this point, what are some of the things you would ask for that you didn't or haven't asked for and why?

SON: What are some of the things you want or need, but haven't yet asked for?

LESSON 16

DAD: How have Judeo-Christian virtues such as honesty, prudence, courage, personal responsibility, private charity, service, hard work, and thrift been a blessing to our country?

SON: Why do you suppose it was important to Thomas Jefferson that we "bind man down from mischief by the chains of the Constitution"?

LESSON 17

DAD: Share an example or two of times when you spoke without thinking and paid the price.

SON: What did King Solomon mean when he said, "Death and life are in the power of the tongue" (Prov. 18:21 KJV)?

LESSON 18

DAD: What are three Bible verses you have memorized or would like to memorize and why did you pick these three?

SON: How does memorizing Scripture help you discipline your mind?

LESSON 19

DAD: What are some goals you have written down and established for your life?

SON: In what ways is grocery shopping similar to life?

LESSON 20

DAD: How have you used the extra-mile principle as a husband, in your career, or in some other aspect of your life?

SON: How could you apply the extra-mile principle to school work, sports, or your family life?

LESSON 21

DAD: How has confidence or a lack of confidence influenced your decision making over the years?

SON: Why does achievement alone not guarantee high levels of self confidence?

LESSON 22

DAD: Throughout your life, have you focused more on being well-rounded or more on building your strengths, and why?

SON: Why do you think great athletes emphasize strength building far more than weakness fixing?

LESSON 23

DAD: Who are the wisest people you spend time with on a regular basis?

SON: Why do you suppose is it typically easier to be pulled down than lifted up?

LESSON 24

DAD: What did President Roosevelt mean when he said, "Any man who says he is an American, but something else also, isn't an American at all"?

SON: What's the connection between individual character and our national character, and why does it matter?

LESSON 25

DAD: What are the three most productive habits you currently possess?

SON: What are two new daily habits that would help you hit your goals over the next year?

LESSON 26

DAD: In what ways have you been exposed to pornography in the past and why are you committed to staying away from it in the future?

SON: In light of the fact that countless men, women, teenagers, and even ministers have all become addicted to porn, how can you protect yourself in a culture that accepts it?

LESSON 27

DAD: In what ways have you intentionally taught your son to recognize truth in a culture that celebrates relativity?

SON: How do you keep focused on truth when you are living in a world of untruth and half-truths?

LESSON 28

DAD: What aspects of your prayer life do you want your son to emulate, and why?

SON: What are the different ways you pray and connect with God?

LESSON 29

DAD: In what ways have you been a faithful steward, and in what ways have you been irresponsible or less than faithful?

SON: How could you be a better steward of your existing talents, opportunities, and other blessings?

LESSON 30

DAD: What life lessons have you learned from *both* winning and losing?

SON: What kind of country would America be if every student made the dean's list and every athlete earned a medal?

LESSON 31

DAD: What lessons have you already taught your son about money, and what essential wisdom do you still need to share?

SON: What is the connection between creating value and earning money, and how old do you need to be for this dynamic to kick in?

LESSON 32

DAD: In what ways have you dreamed big dreams, and in what areas do you wish you had dreamed bigger?

SON: What's the most magnificent goal you can envision yourself reaching?

LESSON 33

DAD: What are the most important truths you've shared with your son about choosing his future spouse and the realities of married life?

SON: What do you think it might be like to be married, and why do you think about half of marriages end in divorce?

LESSON 34

DAD: Since life is a mixture of good and bad, how do you stay positive and optimistic on a day-to-day basis?

SON: What are five things that are awesome about your life right now, and how does that make you feel?

LESSON 35

DAD: Look back over your life and consider: in what ways have you simply gone through the motions and in what ways have you lived with passion?

SON: If you had to do something productive all day long but could choose what that would be, what would you choose?

LESSON 36

DAD: What is your favorite excuse or the excuse that you use most consistently?

SON: Why do you think athletic coaches seem to have a low tolerance for excuses?

LESSON 37

DAD: Describe the price you paid and the seeds you planted to get where you are today in your career, family, financial, and spiritual life.

SON: How does the principle of sowing and reaping help you predict the future?

LESSON 38

DAD: In what ways have you introduced the principles of the free market to your son?

SON: How does a server in an American restaurant demonstrate the virtue of the free market?

LESSON 39

DAD: What aspect of your life could benefit from some added humility?

SON: What is the connection between gratitude and humility?

LESSON 40

DAD: What are the 80/20 truths in your line of work, and how could you use this insight to be more productive?

SON: What are the few things that seem to matter disproportionately more in school, sports, and family life?

LESSON 41

DAD: In what ways are societal problems really character problems, and why does this perspective matter?

SON: How might your choices today as a teenager contribute to a better future for you and your generation?

LESSON 42

DAD: How has your example caused your son to be either more or less compassionate toward others?

SON: In what ways could you extend more compassion to family, friends, teachers, coaches, and even strangers?

LESSON 43

DAD: Where are you in life compared to where you really want to be?

SON: In what areas should you be more brutally honest with yourself or acknowledge a self-defeating mistake or poor choice?

LESSON 44

DAD: What is the single most important project or priority you should start working on daily for fifteen minutes?

SON: How could you put The Fifteen to work for school, for sports, or for your spiritual life?

LESSON 45

DAD: In what areas of your life are you most disciplined and least disciplined, and what have been the consequences of each?

SON: What area of your life could most benefit from some additional discipline, and why?

LESSON 46

DAD: What is the right balance between stewardship of God's resources and the obsession with saving the planet, Earth Day, and other secular initiatives?

SON: What is the difference between legitimate stewardship of the planet and obsessive "earth worship"?

LESSON 47

DAD: When have you engaged with someone's story and learned something unexpected from that person, and how did it influence you?

SON: Have you ever met someone and formed an opinion about him or her, then learned something surprising about that person that taught you something interesting or powerful?

LESSON 48

DAD: When all is said and done, what do you want your life to have stood for?

SON: What three things do you want to create in your life, and what three things do you most want to avoid?

LESSON 49

DAD: What have you done or could you do in the near future to help your son to become "street smart"?

SON: Which is the better indicator of intelligence: the grades you make in school or the choices you make in the rest of your life?

LESSON 50

DAD: What do positive expectations and faith have in common?

SON: How do positive expectations influence performance in sports, schoolwork, and life?

LESSON 51

DAD: Should the government be in charge of making life fair, and if so, who should define what *fair* means?

SON: Do you believe freedom or fairness is the more important American value, and why?

LESSON 52

DAD: What personal experiences with forgiveness should you share with your son?

SON: In what ways do you practice forgiveness on a regular basis, and is there anyone you need to forgive at the moment?

LESSON 53

DAD: Share a few experiences with your son where something felt right or true but ended up being neither.

SON: Looking back, what is one good decision you've made that felt bad at the time and what is one bad decision you've made that felt good at the time?

LESSON 54

DAD: What are some of the ways you deliberately think about God on a regular basis?

SON: In what ways could you spend more time thinking about God in the next week?

LESSON 55

DAD: As a teenager, what did you learn in school about socialism?

SON: What is the connection between socialism, dependence on government, and dependence on God?

LESSON 56

DAD: What has your son learned about integrity from living with and observing you?

SON: Why do you think integrity is often referred to as an "all-or-nothing" quality of character?

LESSON 57

DAD: In what ways could you incorporate or more overtly emphasize grace in your family culture?

SON: How might you explain the concept of grace to someone who has never heard of it before?

LESSON 58

DAD: In what ways have you equipped your son to deal effectively with the inevitable adversities of life?

SON: What has been the toughest time of your life so far, and what did you learn about yourself and adversity in the process?

LESSON 59

DAD: How might political correctness be changing the way we think by changing the way we speak?

SON: In what ways might political correctness limit freedom of speech and diminish independent thinking?

LESSON 60

DAD: What process do you use to regularly evaluate your progress in life, and have you shared this with your son?

SON: How could a little bit of reflection improve your performance academically, athletically, or in any endeavor?

LESSON 61

DAD: How does a victim mind-set erode personal responsibility and contribute to mediocrity?

SON: What is the connection between victimitis, personal responsibility, and excuse making?

LESSON 63

DAD: Why do you suppose world-class athletes and entertainers take advantage of visualization, but the rest of the population rarely does?

SON: How could you incorporate mental rehearsal or the previewing of the goals and dreams you hope to achieve?

LESSON 64

DAD: In what ways is the "everything counts" mind-set already ingrained in your family culture?

SON: How could you make more progress toward your goals by putting into practice the "everything counts" mind-set?

ACKNOWLEDGMENTS

This book reflects the hard work and creativity of many people!

Thank you to Pamela Harty for connecting this project with Thomas Nelson. And thanks to Brian Hampton for believing in the importance of *I Call Shotgun*. We especially appreciate Kristen Parrish and Heather Skelton for their feedback and suggestions that elevated this manuscript to the next level. Thank you, Shelly Beach, for not only helping us finish the manuscript on time, but for adding great perspective as well. Additional thanks to those "behind the scenes" folks at Thomas Nelson who put their talents to use packaging *I Call Shotgun* in exceptional fashion.

We are grateful that our wives, Kristin and Lori, joyfully put up with the late evenings and numerous weekends of writing, and for our sons: Ty, Mason, Brooks, Trey, and Zach, who inspired us to capture our convictions and pass them down while we still had the opportunity.

Never-ending thanks go to each of our parents, whose wisdom, love, and encouragement will outlast them and be a perpetual blessing in the lives of their grandsons and their families for generations to come.

Foremost, we want to thank our heavenly Father for the opportunity and inspiration to write about the things that matter most.

ABOUT THE AUTHORS

Tommy Newberry is the founder and head coach of The 1% Club, a life-coaching firm helping entrepreneurs maximize their full potential across all areas of life. Since 1991, Tommy has equipped business leaders in more than thirty industries to leverage their strengths, maximize their influence, and enjoy greater satisfaction with the right accomplishments. Beyond just business, his annual Couples Planning Retreat and Big Picture Parenting programs help husbands, wives, and parents clarify and stay focused on what matters most.

He is the author of the *New York Times* bestseller *The 4:8 Principle, 40 Days to a Joy-Filled Life*, the motivational classic *Success Is Not an Accident*, and *The War on Success*. Tommy has appeared on over two hundred radio and television shows and is frequently invited to speak at business conferences, schools, and parenting groups. He lives in Atlanta, Georgia, with his wife, Kristin, and their three boys.

Curt Beavers is the president of Network Support Enterprises and one of the top distributors of Juice Plus worldwide. With hundreds of millions in sales, what started as a small, family-run business now has a leadership team of one hundred and over forty thousand distributors across twenty countries. Using biblical principles, and despite current economic conditions, Network Support Enterprises recently finished its fifteenth consecutive year of double-digit growth.

More than dollars and cents, Curt's overriding passion is using business as a platform for ministry. From weekly mentoring and coaching of his own leadership team to hosting annual prayer breakfasts with over four thousand in attendance, Curt's driving force is bringing the gospel to the business world. An instructor with Walk Thru the Bible, Curt speaks to thousands annually both inside and outside his core business.

He is also the founder of Health@College, which brings better health to college students coast to coast, as well as Dorm Based Business, which mentors aspiring entrepreneurs. Most recently, Curt is preparing to launch Charity Dollar—a new fund-raising concept with the goal of perpetually raising one dollar per month from one million individuals.

In 1994, Curt served on the Georgia Board for Promise Keepers and, subsequently, the committee that brought Promise Keepers to the Georgia Dome. When the Olympics came to Atlanta, he was a part of Quest '96, a strategic evangelical event to reach nonbelievers from around the world as they visited Atlanta for the Olympic Games. He and his oldest son have also collaborated to bring large numbers of fathers and sons through the JH Ranch curriculum in California.

Married for twenty-five years and a graduate of Georgia Tech, Curt lives just outside Atlanta with his wife, Lori, and their three children. They worship at Grace Fellowship Church in Snellville, Georgia, where he also serves as an elder.

NOTES

Chapter 1

1. Peter Drucker, as quoted in Dotn Dinkmeyer and Daniel Eckstein, *Leadership by Encouragement* (Boca Raton, FL: CRC Press, 1995).
2. http://thinkexist.com/quotation/whenever_you_see_a _successful_business-someone/167688.html.

Chapter 4

1. http://thinkexist.com/quotation/he_is_a_wise_man_who _does_not_grieve_for_the/147578.html.

Chapter 5

1. http://www.divorcerate.org/.
2. http://frac.org/initiatives/hunger-and-obesity /obesity-in-the-us/.
3. http://www.upi.com/Health_News/2010/05/06/41-percent -of-Americans-will-get-cancer/UPI-75711273192042/.
4. http://www.fool.com/retirement/general/2012/10/15/17 -frightening-facts-about-retirement-savings-in-.aspx.

Chapter 9

1. http://faculty.washington.edu/chudler/what.html.
2. http://www.apologeticspress.org/apcontent .aspx?category=12&article=1345.
3. Ibid. See also William Beck, *Human Design* (New York: Harcourt, Brace, Jovanovich, 1971), 189.

Chapter 11

1. Tommy Newberry, *366 Days of Wisdom & Inspiration* (Mason Press, 2001), 147.

Chapter 12

1. http://quotationsbook.com/quote/1039/.
2. http://thinkexist.com/quotation/when_one_door_closes -another_opens-but_we_often/12671.html.

Chapter 16

1. http://www.princeton.edu/~tjpapers/kyres/kydraft .html#note23b.

Chapter 19

1. Personal interview with the author, January 2012.

Chapter 20

1. http://www.powerhomebiz.com/vol76/walton.htm.
2. http://www.heros-salute.com/Motivation_Zone/motivation _zone_awards.html.

Chapter 22

1. http://www.goodreads.com/quotes/101458-everybody-is-a -genius-but-if-you-judge-a-fish.

Chapter 23

1. http://americanhistory.about.com/cs/georgewashington/a /quotewashington.htm.

Chapter 24

1. Theodore Roosevelt on Immigration, 1907, http://ireport.cnn .com/docs/DOC-47191.

Chapter 25

1. http://dailysuccessquotes.com/Dr_Stephen_Covey.html.
2. http://www.vlib.us/amdocs/texts/prichard38.html.

CHAPTER 26

1. www.safefamilies.org.

CHAPTER 31

1. http://thinkexist.com/quotation/for_it_is_in_giving_that_we_receive/14808.html.

CHAPTER 32

1. http://thinkexist.com/quotation/life_is_too_short_to_be_little-man_is_never_so/258493.html.
2. http://www.brainyquote.com/quotes/authors/c/claude_m_bristol.html.
3. http://quotationsbook.com/quote/40763/.
4. http://www.brainyquote.com/quotes/quotes/h/henrydavid145971.html.

CHAPTER 37

1. As a Man Thinketh, http://jamesallen.wwwhubs.com/think.htm.
2. http://www.intimacywithgod.com/success.html.

CHAPTER 39

1. http://thinkexist.com/quotation/talent_is_god_given-be_humble-fame_is_man-given/148168.html.

CHAPTER 49

1. http://thinkexist.com/quotation/we_are_all_born_ignorant-but_one_must_work_hard/326829.html.
2. http://www.brainyquote.com/quotes/quotes/f/friedricha201836.html.

CHAPTER 55

1. Charles Francis Adams, ed., *The Works of John Adams*, 10 vols. (Boston: Little, Brown and Company, 1850–56), 6:9, 280.
2. Richard Theodore Ely, *Recent American Socialism*, Vol. 3, 1888, 9.
3. http://www.cato.org/publications/commentary/private-property-saved-jamestown-it-america.

4. Richard J. Maybury, "The Great Thanksgiving Hoax," *Mises Daily*, November 20, 1999, http://mises.org/daily/336.

5. Ibid. See also William Bradford, *Bradford's History of the Plymouth Settlement* (New York: E.P. Dutton & Co.), 115 in note 16.

6. William Bradford, *Bradford's History of the Plymouth Settlement* (New York: E.P. Dutton & Co.), 115

7. Ibid.

8. http://www.brainyquote.com/quotes/quotes/w/winstonchu164131.html.

Chapter 56

1. Lou Holtz, "Do Right," Washington Speakers Bureau, 1988.

2. http://thinkexist.com/quotation/character_is_what_you_are_in_the_dark/203799.html.

Chapter 61

1. http://thinkexist.com/quotation/don-t_let_what_you_cannot_do_interfere_with_what/210155.html.